# Pathway

# to the

# Presidency

## Community College
## Deans of Instruction

*by*

# George B. Vaughan

The Community College Press
A Division of the American Association
of Community and Junior Colleges

# Pathway to the Presidency

Published by The Community College Press, a division of the American Association
of Community and Junior Colleges
National Center for Higher Education
One Dupont Circle, N.W., Suite 410
Washington, D.C. 20036
(202) 728-0200

ISBN-87117-200-3

Library of Congress Catalog Card Number: 89-085382

To Peggy

*The Best*

# Contents

■

# *Preface*

■

In 1966 I took a leave of absence from my position as an instructor of history at a branch campus of Virginia Polytechnic Institute and State University to return to graduate school to work on a Ph.D. in history. While I was in graduate school, the state of Virginia passed legislation creating a system of public community colleges. The branch campus where I had been employed was to be absorbed into the community college system prior to my return.

Don Puyear, the director of the branch campus and the soon-to-be president of the soon-to-be community college, asked if he could pay me a visit. The purpose of his visit was not to inquire about the progress of my Ph.D.; rather, he came to ask me to be the dean of instruction at the newly created community college. My response: "What is a dean of instruction?" His response to my response: "I'll be damned if I know, but if you want the position, we'll find out together."

Two deanships, two presidencies, a Ph.D. in higher education rather than history, and over two and a half decades later I am prepared at least partially to answer the question I posed so innocently and so long ago: "What is a dean of instruction?"

Much has happened over the past three decades to the community college. Playing a key role in the development of these institutions has been, is, and likely will be the dean of instruction. Indeed, president after president with whom I have talked agree that to have an outstanding community college one must have an outstanding dean of instruction.

In spite of the importance of the dean of instruction's position, however, very little is known about the individuals who occupy these critical positions. What are their family backgrounds? Academic preparation? Perceptions of their roles? And what does the future hold for the community college as many of the current deans move into the presidency of these institutions? These, and a number of other questions, will be addressed in the following pages. In addition to providing answers, a number of questions will be posed, especially to those individuals responsible for employing the future leaders of these important institutions.

## DEFINITION OF TERMS

The title "dean of instruction" is used to designate the person responsible for the instructional program at the community college, or, stated another way, the institution's chief academic officer. Some colleges use the title academic dean; larger ones often use academic vice-president. While titles vary from state to state and from campus to campus, the most common title tends to be dean of instruction, the one I have chosen to use in this study. Occasionally, in order to avoid repeating dean of instruction each time, I will use the term academic dean, chief academic officer, deanship, or simply dean when discussing the dean of instruction.

The term "community college" includes public two-year technical colleges and public junior colleges as well as public community colleges. Only public institutions are discussed in this study.

"President" is used to refer to the chief executive officer of a public community, junior, or technical college. As is the case with the dean of instruction's position, the chief executive's title varies and includes chancellor, director, and superintendent-president.

## METHODOLOGY

A number of approaches were used in conducting the study. I drew upon my own brief experiences as a dean of instruction at two community colleges and upon my extensive experience (17 years) as a community college president.

A "Career and Lifestyles Survey" (CLS) almost identical to the one I used in developing parts of the book, *The Community College Presidency* (Vaughan, 1986), was sent to the individuals identified by the American Association of Community and Junior Colleges (AACJC) as the chief academic officers of public community, junior, and technical colleges. Gathering essentially the same type of information on the deans of instruction that I gathered on the presidents provided a basis of comparison between the two groups. Part of the information gathered from the survey of the deans was used in a chapter in my second volume on the community college presidency, titled *Leadership in Transition: The Community College Presidency* (Vaughan, 1989b).

In separate surveys, I surveyed female, Black, and Hispanic deans. These surveys were essentially duplicates of the ones I used to survey female, Black, and Hispanic presidents, again providing a basis of comparison between the deans and the presidents. The results of the presidential surveys are reported in *Leadership in Transition* (Vaughan, 1989b).

Those deans identified as leaders also were surveyed regarding their views on the dean's position. The survey used was essentially the same as the one used to survey presidents identified as leaders by their peers, the results of which were reported in *The Community College Presidency* (Vaughan, 1986). As above, by using essentially the same survey, the deans identified as leaders can be compared with the presidents so identified even though the method of selecting deans to participate in the survey differed from the method used to survey presidents identified as leaders by their peers.

I conducted extensive interviews with 15 deans of instructions from 13 different states. A major purpose of the interviews was to offer the deans an opportunity to discuss their positions in more detail than was possible on the survey form.

Whereas with the study of the presidency I found a number of sources dealing with the subject, most with the four-year college presidency, I found very little published on the community college's dean of instruction; therefore, the references dealing directly with the subject of this volume are limited. Nevertheless, a search of the literature on the subject was conducted and the sources used, where applicable. I did not, however, attempt to track down dissertations dealing with the dean of instruction's position.

## OVERVIEW

Chapter 1 provides an overview of the role of the dean of instruction. Included in this chapter are definitions of the dean of instruction's position. Special emphasis is placed on the role of the dean as the institution's chief academic officer.

Chapter 2 provides an intimate profile of current deans of instruction. Family background is discussed, as is educational background. This chapter compares current deans with current presidents in a number of areas. Are current deans mirror images of current presidents? If so, so what?

Chapter 3 examines the pathway to the deanship. Division chairs often become deans of instruction. What are some other avenues to the deanship? Included in this chapter is a discussion of some of the things the deans were not prepared to face upon assuming the position.

Chapter 4 discusses the frustrations and satisfactions derived from being a female dean of instruction, including looking at some of the obstacles faced by some women on the pathway to the deanship. The question, "Is the dean of instruction's position asexual?" is answered.

Chapter 5 approaches Black deans in much the same way as Chapter 4 approaches female deans. Black deans are asked if the dean's position is aracial? And, if not, why not?

Chapter 6 continues to look at minority deans, covering much of the same ground with Hispanic deans that is covered with female and Black deans. All three chapters are important in understanding the community college as well as the dean's position.

Chapter 7 is devoted to leadership. In this chapter the views of the deans are compared with those of community college presidents. The similarities between the two groups are striking.

Chapter 8 offers advice for those who have the dean of instruction's position as a career goal and for deans who have as a career goal the community college presidency. Included is a discussion of how one can enhance one's chances of becoming a dean and a president. This chapter can be especially important to those deans who have not developed a clear career path leading to the presidency.

Chapter 9 concludes the volume with a series of conclusions and recommendations, including some recommendations from deans to presidents on how presidents can more effectively work with deans of instruction. The chapter also includes some things that deans want from presidents.

# Acknowledgments

∎

I am sincerely grateful for the many chief academic officers who returned the various surveys that generated much of the data used in this book. A special note of thanks is due to those deans who shared their time and knowledge during the interviews. Special assistance was given by Betty Duvall and Sharon Yaap, both of whom cooperated in every way possible with the study. Karen Bowyer was generous with her support and encouragement. Gustavo Mellander and Alfredo de los Santos were helpful in identifying the Hispanic deans; Richard Turner was equally helpful in identifying Black deans. In regard to the latter, a special note of thanks to Belle Wheelan, an intelligent, tireless leader.

Don Puyear was extremely helpful in analyzing the data from the Career and Lifestyle Survey. He remains a good colleague and friend.

Jim Palmer was an unlimited source of information who offered criticism when warranted and encouragement always. His insights were especially valuable in developing the summaries for the various chapters and in assisting with the surveys and data analysis. He also encouraged the study while a vice-president with the AACJC.

Bonnie Gardner and Susan Reneau of the AACJC staff were responsible for finally bringing the book together. They are outstanding professionals in a most demanding segment of the profession. Of course, the book could not have come about without the support of Dale Parnell and Jim Gollattscheck.

Lou Klaric, co-author of Chapter 4, became my graduate assistant at a time when the project was mired in my mind and beginning to get lost among my priorities. Lou is a tireless worker, an excellent copy editor, and a devoted professional. Her co-authorship of the chapter on female deans brought the valuable perspective of a woman to the chapter. Simply stated, the book would not have been completed on time if Lou had not joined the project.

Every successful operation must have that one individual who holds things together, no matter what the circumstances. The Center for Community College Education is indeed fortunate to have Brenda Noel in that role, for she is a caring, intelligent, hard-working individual whose support and friendship are always given freely. She also proofreads with an eagle eye. Thank you Brenda for your patience, support, and for just caring. It is a pleasure and honor to work with you.

Peggy Vaughan, here we go again. What can I say about you that I haven't said before? As always, you were great throughout the writing of this volume; you remain the best editor I have ever had the privilege to work with. Brandt and Andrew gave their usual support, encouragement, and love. As a family, we make a good team, a team I am honored to be a member of.

—George B. Vaughan

# PART I

∎

*The Setting*

P art I of this volume (Chapters 1–3) provides the setting for the remainder of the volume. In this section, a very brief look is taken at the evolution of the dean of instruction's position, including a rationale as to why the title itself is important. Current deans of instruction offer their definitions of the position. The deans' definitions, in conjunction with the few sources that were available and examined, provide the reader with an overview of the dean of instruction's position in the total scheme of community college education.

Part I also provides a number of statistics and information on those individuals who currently occupy the dean's position, including information on the deans' family background. Much of the information on the deans' background came from my Career and Lifestyle Survey, referred to in the remainder of the study as the CLS, which was sent to the deans for data collection purposes (See Appendix 1). A number of deans discuss what influence, if any, family background has on the way they view the dean's position.

Finally, in order to provide the setting for the remainder of the volume, the pathway to the deanship is examined in some detail. Selected deans discuss how well-prepared they believe they were upon assuming the deanship. Frustrations and satisfactions are a part of all professional positions; the dean of instruction's position is no exception, as a number of deans acknowledge. When helpful, the dean of instruction's position is compared with the community college presidency. The reader may be shocked to find how closely current deans of instruction resemble current presidents. With this in mind, a question the readers might ponder as they read this first section is what the future community college presidency will look like, assuming a number of the current deans will be future presidents.

# 1

# An Overview

■

I n the preface to this volume, the question "What is a dean of instruction?" is asked. A first step in answering this question is to define the term.

The dean of instruction is defined in this study as the institution's chief academic officer, that person who is responsible for faculty
recruitment and development and program identification and development, and who has the overall responsibility for the institution's academic program. The dean of instruction reports directly to the president
of the institution and is a member of the president's administrative team.
The dean of instruction's major constituencies are the teaching faculty
and those administrators, such as division chairs, who provide support
for the institution's academic program, and ultimately the students.

Titles are important, I believe. On the community college campus,
the dean of instruction is the counterpart of the academic vice-president
or provost at four-year institutions. The temptation was to title this study
"The Academic Dean," rather than "The Dean of Instruction," in order
to comply with the more popular terminology used by much of academia. To have done so would have, however, run the risk of having some
readers confuse the dean of instruction's position with more traditional
deans, such as the dean of arts and sciences, although in most institutions that have deans of schools and colleges, it is clear that they head

a segment of the academic program and report to a provost or academic vice-president who is the institution's chief academic officer.

Defining the community college's chief academic officer as the dean of instruction immediately opens doors of confusion, for the title given to the chief academic officer in community colleges varies from campus to campus. For example, some campuses use the title of dean for other positions that report to the chief academic officer, especially on larger campuses where titles such as vice-president and provost are used. Titles used by community colleges for the chief academic officer include academic dean, academic vice-president, vice-president for instruction, instructional dean, dean of the college, and any number of other titles that are used at a particular college at a particular point in time. In addition, community colleges often use the title "provost" to designate the head of a campus in multi-campus or multi-college operations; in many cases, the provost also serves as the chief academic officer for the campus. Definitions aside, however, each institution recognizes its chief academic officer as the person responsible for the institution's academic programs, the academic leader who works directly with the faculty. As one source notes, the chief academic officer must have a view of the "academic health of the entire campus," including determining if there are "soft spots" in the curriculum, a productive and satisfied faculty, and support services that help to create an atmosphere in which students can reach their potential (Wolverton, 1984, pp. 13-14).

## AN EMERGING TITLE

A 1973 survey of all of the deans of public community colleges found that 48 percent of the chief academic officers had the title of dean of instruction (Anderson, 1973). Another study conducted 12 years later found that in the state of Kansas 84 percent of the chief academic officers used the title "dean of instruction" (Parker & Parker, 1985); in Virginia, the official title for the chief academic officer at the state's 23 community colleges is dean of instruction, although recently a number of colleges have combined student services and instruction under the ubiquitous title "dean of the college," a position that encompasses admissions, thereby making the responsibilities of the dean of the college resemble more closely those of the provost at some four-year institutions.

Today, "dean of instruction" seems to be the most common title used by community colleges to designate the individual on campus who has the major responsibility for the institution's instructional program, including faculty matters. While titles varied, everyone interviewed for this study understood the term "dean of instruction," although those with titles such as vice-president were careful to refer to their position by its correct title, giving the impression that they feel the title "vice-president" carries more prestige and responsibility than does that of "dean of instruction." Nevertheless, the community college popularized the title "dean of instruction," making it its own, and thereby making it even more appropriate to use the title "dean of instruction" for this study.

Until the community college popularized the term, the title "dean of instruction," while not unknown, was somewhat alien to higher education's lexicon. Indeed, one study conducted in 1973 on the dean of instruction's position noted that "the researcher set out to ascertain and examine the characteristics, preparation, and attitudes of a very new two-year college administrator. Had the same study been conducted 10 years earlier, the results would certainly have shown that the chief academic officer was the president" (Anderson, 1973, p. 2). (Maybe my question asked in 1966, "What is a dean of instruction?" was not so naive after all.) Those individuals who attended college in the 1950s and before recognize such titles as dean of men, dean of women, and academic dean or dean of faculties. Later generations recognize such terms as academic vice-president, provost, or simply dean as designating the institution's academic leader, although at universities made up of colleges and schools, the dean normally is in charge of a school (school of engineering) or college (college of arts and sciences) and reports to an academic vice-president or provost. Few of either generation were exposed to the title "dean of instruction" until community colleges popularized the term.

No attempt was made to trace the origins of the title. One can speculate on how the term evolved, however. As is well known, early community colleges emerged as something of a hybrid, drawing heavily from the public high school and from higher education. A common title in some public school systems during the 1950s and 1960s was director of instruction. The title "dean" was an accepted term in American higher education by the early twentieth century. One can speculate, then, that community colleges may have borrowed the title "dean" from higher education and that of "instruction" from public schools, thus the title "dean of instruction." On the other hand, some four-year institutions, including some former teachers colleges, used (and some few still do) the title "dean of instruction" for their chief academic officer, thus suggesting that the title was borrowed directly from higher education. My observations regarding the origin of the title are pure speculation and are likely to raise more questions than provide answers; moreover, whether tracing the origin of the use of the title in community colleges would shed light on the development of these colleges in America also is subject to conjecture.

More important than offering a definition for the term "dean of instruction" or tracing the origins of the title, however, is an understanding of the role at the community college, thereby partially answering the question: What is a dean of instruction?

## BACKGROUND

A brief ERIC topical paper published in 1974 discusses the role of the dean of instruction at one community college. The study was written by William F. Shawl, who at the time of the publication was dean of instruction (he used the title "academic dean" for himself and in the title of the topical paper) at Golden West College, California. The author makes it clear that his study is not a "highly-researched, well-validated study of the role of the academic dean" (p. v), but rather it is "the impressions and ideas of one dean of seven years' experience" (p. v). Nevertheless, Shawl's brief study provides a benchmark in the evolution of the dean of instruction's position and is useful in placing the position in perspective.

Shawl (1974) cites studies that assigned at least 41 duties to the dean of instruction; one dissertation he cites developed a comprehensive list of 168 duties associated with the position. Even after listing 168 duties, the study concluded that deans of instruction lack a clearly defined set of duties and, moreover, are required to perform duties that are not compatible with the position (p. 1). Turning to another dissertation that asked deans to rank a series of 78 selected duties in terms of importance, Shawl reported that the deans ranked in order of importance and as extremely important: (1) coordinating and supervising instructional departments and divisions; (2) formulating educational policy; (3) interpreting and administering academic policies; (4) recommending or approving personnel actions, including promotions and dismissals; (5) recommending faculty appointments, assignments, and salaries; and (6) providing for faculty participation in developing curricula (p. 2). Shawl observed that, in their daily lives, deans rarely stop to think about a job description; rather, "The most immediate things are the relationships that exist between the dean and the individuals and groups that he deals with in his leadership role" (p. 2). (Shawl's observation was borne out time and again in the interviews I conducted with deans of instruction.)

In words as relevant today (and words that will win the hearts of all current deans of instruction) as they were in 1974, Shawl captured the complexity of the role of the dean of instruction in dealing with an ever increasing number of external and internal forces.

It takes a very persistent and skillful dean to steer a new program through a local advisory committee, the campus curriculum committee, the regional planning committee, the local board of trustees and, finally, the state chancellor's office. After working with all of these decision-making and advisory groups, one really wonders if he is providing leadership in curriculum development. Others seem to be in control of the resources needed for the program's success, and they (not the dean) are really determining which programs will be tried and which will not. The dean plays the persuader-politician role to get the new curriculum which he and his faculty colleagues feel is essential for students (p. 3).

• • •

In considering the above, the reader should keep the date it was written in mind and realize that the author was the dean at a California community college, a state that prides itself (more so in 1974 than today) on local control of its community colleges.

To conclude the discussion from Shawl (1974), he saw three major roles for the dean of instruction: (1) interpreter/mediator of policies and procedures; (2) advocate for the instructional needs of the college; and (3) instructional leader of the institution. His conclusion is that "The central focus of the academic dean's role will be as it has always been—instructional leadership" (p. 16).

In a recent publication I discussed the role of the dean of instruction.[1] In my discussion I cited the example of a dean of instruction who had been directed by a state agency to contact his counterparts at 15 four-year institutions, ranging in size and prestige from one with fewer than 1,000 students to two major research universities with a large number of deans (one had an academic vice-president and another had a provost in charge of the academic program) and very complex organizational structures. His frustrations grew out of trying to decide just who would be viewed as his counterparts at the four-year colleges and universities. The purpose of contacting his "counterparts" was to discuss transfer issues

---

[1]My previous analysis of the role of the dean of instruction is found in *Leadership in Transition: The Community College Presidency*. New York: ACE/Macmillan, 1989, pp. 109–123. Much of the following discussion is taken from this volume.

between two- and four-year institutions. Who, in dealing with transfer issues, are my "counterparts?" the dean asked, for most universities to which community college students transfer require that students be admitted to a specific school or college, such as the college of arts and sciences or the school of engineering. Schools and colleges have deans; one of the universities in the state had six who might be viewed by a state agency as counterparts to the dean of instruction. Had this dean of instruction followed directions and contacted those who might be viewed as his counterparts by those individuals unfamiliar with community colleges, he would have had to contact approximately 38 individuals at eight universities and at least seven other individuals at the remaining institutions.

An understanding of the role of the dean of instruction, as is true with so much else in the development of the community college, has often been gradual and somewhat by trial and error. Nevertheless, most faculty members in a community college know more about the dean of instruction's position than they do about other administrative positions such as the presidency if for no other reason than that they work more closely with the dean than with the president. Nevertheless, the above example regarding the request for transfer information gives an indication of some of the complexities inherent in understanding the dean of instruction's position in a community college, a position that is in some ways unique to these colleges and in other ways similar to other positions of academic leadership in higher education.

In an earlier discussion of the dean of instruction, I made an effort to describe the role, placing emphasis on the broader aspects of the position. My description follows:

> For example, deans of instruction at community colleges perform most of the duties assigned to the chief academic officer at small, four-year private colleges; deans of instruction perform many of the duties performed by provosts or academic vice-presidents at major universities; they perform many of the duties performed by the deans of the various schools or colleges within major universities (i.e., passing judgment on faculty for tenure and promotions); and many deans of instruction oversee the college's continuing education program, a function performed by deans of continuing education at most colleges and universities with a continuing education division. Deans of instruction even perform some of the functions assigned to deans of professional schools (i.e., accreditation and licensure) in those community colleges with nursing and other health programs. To summarize, deans of

instruction deal daily with college-wide issues; pass professional judgment on all teaching faculty; report to and advise the college president; are responsible for the college's programs of study and schedule of classes; help with long-range planning; work with the college's public relations program; plan, monitor, and spend a budget; deal with external agencies; and, in general, have their fingers on the pulse beat of the entire college in a way that is equalled only by the college president. The successful dean of instruction must be a leader with vision, a manager of details, an advocate of the faculty, and a representative of the president's office. Indeed, the dean of instruction's position probably requires more time, energy, and attention to a myriad of details than any other administrative position on campus, including that of president. Significantly, the dean of instruction is the only individual on campus who deals with the entire academic program on a day-to-day basis. The dean of instruction has responsibility to ensure that the college does not stray from its central mission of teaching and learning. Ultimately, the effective dean of instruction serves as an 'internal auditor' responsible for maintaining the college's academic integrity (Vaughan, 1989b, pp. 110–111).

• • •

In an interview on the subject of the chief academic officer (Marchese, 1989), Richard Miller discusses the findings of his study on the chief academic officers at four-year and two-year institutions. Among his conclusions is his belief that "There's not much question that [the] CAO [chief academic officer] is the second most important position in any postsecondary institution. Some people say it's number one, but I think the president has a broader set of responsibilities" (p. 3). Miller goes on to note that "there's been very little study of CAOs" (p. 3).

A sourcebook on the role of the chief academic officer, titled *Leadership Roles of Chief Academic Officers* (Brown, 1984), provides insights into the role of the chief academic officer. Particularly helpful in understanding the role is the chapter, "The Chief Academic Officer: Argus on the Campus," by Robert E. Wolverton (1984), vice-president for academic affairs at Mississippi State University at the time the chapter was written.

Wolverton (1984) believes the chief academic officer (CAO) must have the following views: (1) up, to the president and governing board; (2) down, to those administrators who report directly to the chief academic officer; (3) sideways, to peers who are responsible for student services, financial affairs, and similar operations; and (4) oblique, to associate and assistant vice-presidents, associate and assistant deans, and assistants to the president.

> At the same time, the CAO must take a campus view of faculty, students, and curricula; a system view to answer queries on such subjects as duplication of programs, tenure and academic freedom, the quality of students, and the mission of this institution as opposed to that of others in the system; and a national view to be aware of new concerns and issues within the profession in other parts of the country. Finally, for their own sense of survival and well-being, CAOs must occasionally have a review of where they are going, what they are doing, and what they are becoming (Wolverton, 1984, p. 7).

• • •

Wolverton continues: "The CAO, then, like Argus, must have clear and open eyes, for on the CAO's views rest the quality and the reputation of the institution, as well as the satisfaction of students, faculty, and other administrators" (p. 8).

While Wolverton (1984) views the chief academic officer's role from the perspective of a four-year university, he nevertheless captures the essence of the chief academic officer's role at community colleges in his concluding remarks. "In summary, the CAO in every institution of higher education has a unique role: to lead, administer, and manage the people and the ideas that are the lifeblood of the institution.... The Argus-eyed CAO makes a major contribution to the campus and all its concerned constituencies" (pp. 16–17).

## DEANS OF INSTRUCTION DEFINE THEIR POSITION

In an attempt to gain a fuller understanding of the role of the dean of instruction, I asked a number of the deans interviewed for this study to define the position. One dean made a point to avoid giving what he referred to as a "textbook" definition. He views the role of the dean as aiding the instructional divisions in providing instruction to students, including finding the necessary resources; aiding in curriculum development; and serving as an advocate for instruction. He observed: "You have the administrative structure which includes the finance side and the instructional side, and sometimes you have to be a strong advocate to make certain that the academic divisions receive positions and other resources."

Sounding a similar note, another dean believes that the dean is the person who "aids in the leadership of the entire college, which includes the faculty, to develop curriculum through an orderly process and of delivering that curriculum to reach the needs of the student community." A dean whose background prior to moving into administration was art history, while seeing herself responsible for the instructional program, notes that in reality, "I see that it's the faculty that carries out the mission, but I'm responsible for making sure that the appropriate decisions are made as effectively as possible and that the needs of the students are met." Many of the decisions, she notes, deal with requesting and distributing funds, evaluation of programs, scheduling, and staffing. Another dean notes that "one of the major components of the position is working with division directors and gathering their input to implement curricular ideas, directions for the college, program ideas, and that type of thing." Similarly, from another: "My job as academic officer is a leadership role. I like to look at it as the person who is the advocate for the academic area, who breaks down barriers for individuals and the bureaucracy of the institution, whether faculty, division chairpeople who report to me, or other administrators."

A dean who moved through the administrative ranks quickly and who had accepted a presidency at the time I interviewed him, but had not yet reported for his new position, offers the following definition of the dean's position:

> It is a multi-faceted position that varies depending upon the nature of the organization and the kind of skills you bring to it. Basically, I would say it is a leadership position, responsible for directing the instructional leadership of the organization, particularly in terms of faculty, curriculum, and instruction. The effective dean must have the ability to work with people, to motivate people, and to have some sense of direction about what the instructional segment of the organization needs to go toward. I believe the individual has to have some creativity in problem solving and flexibility in terms of solving problems. The individual, I think, also has to have enough foresight to anticipate problems and solve most of them before they become major issues; but most of all, I think that the individual has to have a plan of action to maximize the teaching-learning process, which is the college's primary mission.

• • •

Another dean places emphasis on his role as manager and leader. The dean "is the person who must demonstrate good leadership skills and must also manage a diverse group of individuals through the division chairs." Similarly, from another: "The dean, I would say, is a partner in the leadership of the college, rather than being the leader. I think it's my job to organize and to keep it moving, basically, as a catalyst, not necessarily as the leader. The leader is the composite of you and those people who are forming the same mission." In the same vein, a dean at a technical institution notes that she places a great deal of emphasis on the daily operations of the institution. Beyond assuring quality instruction throughout the institution, she sees her role as "making sure the programs run smoothly and that we have qualified faculty and those types of things." Another dean sees his role simply as an advocate for students and the faculty and as a supporter of the comprehensive community college in his community.

Another dean defines the position in terms of setting and accomplishing goals. The first step is to identify the goals that are important, "being specific where you can, not being afraid if they're too general, but get the goals down." The second step is "to try to motivate and give responsibility to those who are responsible for carrying out the goals."

One dean defines her position rather broadly with emphasis on her role as the instructional leader.

> The dean's position is to provide academic leadership, but at our college, one of the things that may be atypical is that all instruction is combined into one division, including day, evening, regular session, winter, summer, credit, and non-credit—including continuing professional development, avocational and recreational courses—all in one division. So my job is not just academic leadership in the traditional sense but instructional and community services leadership. So I see myself at the center of the comprehensive mission of the community college. I work with full-time faculty, adjunct faculty, and all of the people we call in to do the continuing and professional development as well as avocational instruction.

• • •

One veteran of three deanships defines his role succinctly: "Well, my role has always been that of chief academic officer, and I think that's the most central way to look at it. The dean is the person who is responsible for managing the whole of the curriculum, the whole of the educational offerings, for providing the support necessary for the faculty to do their job, to deliver an effective instructional program."

While working with the president is an important aspect of the dean's position and one that will be discussed in more detail later, one veteran dean, alluding to the importance of planning, budgeting, and working with the faculty, observes that, in the final analysis, "I do everything the president doesn't want to do." According to one dean who has no desire to become a president, to be an effective dean one must be comfortable working in a middle position between the president and the other administrators and faculty. Another dean concludes that the dean's position "varies, depending upon the comfort level of the president you're working for."

## SKILLS AND PERSONAL ATTRIBUTES

The overwhelming set of skills required by the successful dean of instruction is what a number of deans refer to as "people skills." Every dean interviewed alluded to these skills in one way or another.

The following quotes, all from different deans, are representative of what the deans mean by people skills and how these skills are used to serve the institution:

*I think you need to be able to listen to people and to know who they are. I think early in my career I tried to make too many people over to be like me, or like someone else, and now I think you need to be able to say, well, now that person has these skills and abilities. Let's put them on this side of the court because that's where they can do well.*

● ● ●

*The one thing I think [you must have] is interpersonal skills, being able to build a team of individuals who will work together to move the institution, move its curriculum. The interpersonal skills and an understanding of the learning process are important.*

● ● ●

*I think it's good to be a good organizer, to have a vision, be forward-thinking, have a thick skin and a sense of humor. But I think you have to be people-oriented. And I think that's the most important part, because so much of your work is with people, either students, faculty, or other administrators.*

● ● ●

*I think an understanding of what faculty feel is important. I've spent a lot of time talking with faculty, and I think I understand what they* mean when they talk about teaching excellence and other kinds of things. We communicate well together.

• • •

I would say that the strongest skills required are really what we call people skills: working with folks, trying to provide leadership by example, working to bring people together, having an interest in working with people and helping them to achieve the goals they set as you work with them to set those goals.

• • •

I think the best skill that anyone needs to have would be that of the human skill; caring for what you're doing; caring for the people you work with; and respecting those people and knowing that you are a partner in the effort. You can learn the mechanics of the job, but you can't learn how to deal with people and you can't learn good communications skills. You can improve them, but you have to have some of those, and I think you have to be sincere.

• • •

Probably the most important skills I use on a daily basis are my human relations skills—just dealing with people on a day-to-day basis—being able to trouble-shoot and make decisions that will facilitate and help people do their jobs.

• • •

I think the most important things are people skills, certainly listening skills, and the ability to step out, in certain ways, of my role as administrator and be able really to listen to individuals, listen to their problems, and try to assist them in seeking alternative ways to get to whatever their issue is, either resolve it or to expedite what they are trying to do.

• • •

I flippantly tell people that I go to meetings and return phone calls. But I find I spend most of my time dealing with people, and that requires most of my attention. I work with the faculty, developing curriculum, with outreach into the community, relationships with schools and universities, and with business and industry.

• • •

Finally, one dean believes that the more important skills are those used in negotiations and conflict resolution, which are ultimately "people skills." "These are the kinds of skills it takes to deal with faculty who have different goals, with department chairs who may be at odds with each other, getting them to recognize what they have in common. I deal less with students than with faculty and other professionals, but I would say that 'people skills,' in terms of conflict resolution and negotiations, are number one."

One personal attribute that one dean insists is mandatory is having a lot of energy, both physical and mental. Other skills mentioned often are ones that one would expect any successful academic administrator to have: skill in working with a budget; being able to write a proposal; understanding the instructional program; being able to set priorities; and any number of other skills and attributes needed to carry out the duties of the office.

Another dean also alludes to negotiation skills in the more formal sense, for she finds her role shaped by the institution's collective bargaining agreement. She notes:

> Certainly, good management skills are essential because I work in an institution that is under very stringent collective bargaining regulations. It is a statewide contract, versus an individual campus contract, and so, as happens in many institutions, the governance process gets mixed up into collective bargaining issues, and they are looked upon as statewide issues, not institutional issues, so where you would normally be able to resolve a problem through trust between either the division chairperson and the faculty member, the dean and the faculty member, or the president, there is no trust relationship that can be built up because you're dealing with an outside group which is the whole state, and if it becomes an issue on a single campus, you cannot break down that barrier, and I think that's one of the biggest problems.

● ● ●

Her college's way of keeping the personal touch in the administrative process was to break the institution into "mini colleges," thereby permitting her and other administrators to have a "one-to-one relationship with our faculty, rather than a faculty of 100-plus full-time individuals, plus 150 adjunct faculty, all trying to filter toward one individual who is then seen as the person who is implementing the collective bargaining rules and regulations."

## SUMMARY

Despite the pivotal role played by chief academic officers, few researchers have examined the professional lives and responsibilities of these key community college educators. The following conclusions are drawn from the few studies about chief academic officers that have been conducted:

- Titles for the chief academic officer at community colleges vary and include, among others, "dean of instruction," "academic dean," "academic vice-president," and "vice-president for instruction." Regardless of the title, each institution recognizes its chief academic officer as the person who works directly with the faculty and who is responsible for the institution's academic programs.

- Deans of instruction have numerous duties that vary greatly from institution to institution depending, as Shawl (1974) points out, on "the relationship between the dean and the individuals and groups that he deals with in his leadership role" (p. 2). These duties require the dean to bring leadership, management, and interpersonal skills to bear on the task of advocacy for the college's academic program. Indeed, the dean of instruction has the overall responsibility to ensure that the college does not stray from its central mission of teaching and learning.

- In carrying out these duties, deans operate as middlemen in the college, linking faculty work to the educational goals of the president. Deans of instruction are the primary link between the faculty and the college's administration. Success depends largely on the dean's "people skills," a point repeatedly raised in my interviews with deans from across the country.

Regardless of the title, it is no exaggeration to say that the dean of instruction must work well with practically all of the members of the college community, especially faculty. Working with the various campus constituencies requires that the dean have excellent interpersonal skills and an ability to mediate in both formal (unionized) and informal settings (a number of deans referred to the need for negotiating skills). A sense of humor and flexibility in one's approach to the job are as important as good management and planning skills. Working with both administrators and faculty to promote the teaching and learning mission, the effective dean of instruction must view the institution from a broader perspective than was the case before moving into the dean's position.

Who is the dean of instruction? The following chapters will continue to explore this complex question and to provide some additional answers.

# 2

# A Profile of the Dean of Instruction

■

The dean of instruction is critical to the success of the community college, both on individual campuses and nationally. Responsible for the instructional program, these individuals are at the center of what is ultimately of greatest importance to the community college, teaching and learning. Deans of instruction also occupy that middle ground where many of the tensions of the college come together, where daily battles are fought: administrative concerns versus faculty concerns; student services concerns versus instructional concerns; financial concerns for non-instructional activities versus financial concerns for instruction; division chair concerns versus presidential concerns; and the list goes on.

Not even the president's office is subjected to the daily conflicts from so many important segments of the campus community as is the dean of instruction's office (this may not be true on some unionized campuses), for as one source notes, "if you're a CAO, everyone wants a piece of you. That's less the case for a president" (Marchese, 1989, p. 6). The same source observes that presidents are involved in many duties external to the campus such as fund raising and legislative work. "In that sense, the presidency does have escape hatches. Presidents can be off the campus more; they can control their agenda more" (p. 5). Moreover, in contrast to the president who often has the final word in resolving campus tensions, the dean of instruction must deal with other deans as peers and faculty who are, in the best sense of the term, colleagues of the dean. Who are the individuals who occupy these critical positions on campus?

Understanding the dean of instruction's position can be enhanced through exploring the background of those individuals who occupy the position. Moreover, if the past is prologue to the future, a number of current deans of instruction will occupy the president's office in the future. With this in mind, this chapter looks at a number of similarities between the deans and presidents, thereby providing an interesting and perhaps useful perspective for viewing the community college's past, present, and future, for by gaining a better understanding of the two most important leadership positions on campus, one's knowledge and understanding of the community college is increased.

## FAMILY BACKGROUND

In *The Community College Presidency*, I examined the family backgrounds of current presidents in the areas of parental occupations and educational levels, both important indicators of a family's socioeconomic status (Vaughan, 1986, pp. 10–11). In *Leadership in Transition* (Vaughan, 1989b), Chapter 7 is titled "The Next Generation," the thesis of which is that the most important source of community college presidents for the next generation will be current deans of instruction. Drawing upon these two previous works, the present chapter examines the family backgrounds of the deans of instruction, using parental occupations and educational levels as the major socioeconomic indicators of family background.

### Parents' Education

Before addressing the educational levels of the parents of deans of instruction, a brief look at the educational levels of the parents of current presidents provides a basis of comparison between the deans and presidents. The information on the presidents was obtained from a Career and Lifestyles Survey (CLS) sent to 838 presidents of public two-year institutions, to which 591 (70.5 percent) responded. The information is reported in *The Community College Presidency* (Vaughan, 1986). Essentially the same survey was sent to 1,169 chief academic officers of the nation's public two-year colleges; 619 (53 percent) returned the survey. The information on the family backgrounds of deans of instruction was obtained from the CLS and was reported, in part, in *Leadership in Transition* (Vaughan, 1989b, pp. 109–124) and in an article in the *Community,*

*Technical, and Junior College Journal* (Puyear, Perkins, and Vaughan, 1990). The same information was gathered on deans and presidents in order that the two might be compared, thereby increasing one's understanding of both positions and, one would hope, increasing one's understanding of the community college.

Fifty-one percent of the fathers of current community college presidents did not complete high school; another 29 percent finished high school but did not continue their formal education. Stated another way, 80 percent of the fathers of current community college presidents have a high school diploma or less. The educational level of mothers of current presidents, while slightly higher than that of the fathers, is similar. Almost 40 percent of the mothers of current presidents did not finish high school; 38 percent completed high school but did not attend college; therefore, 78 percent of the mothers have a high school diploma or less. My conclusion in *The Community College Presidency* was that, based upon the educational level of their parents, the majority of the current community college presidents came from a working-class or blue-collar background (Vaughan, 1986, pp. 10–11).

Turning now to the deans of instruction, one finds that the fathers and mothers of current deans of instruction are somewhat better educated than are the parents of current presidents. While the difference of those with a high school degree or less is not major, the percentage of high school graduates is significantly higher. Almost 38 percent of the fathers of the deans of instruction have less than a high school diploma; almost 39 percent have a high school diploma but did not attend college; thus, almost 77 percent of the fathers of current deans of instruction have a high school diploma or less. Slightly over 29 percent of the mothers of current deans of instruction have less than a high school diploma; 46.5 percent finished high school but did not attend college; thus, over 75 percent of the mothers of current deans have a high school diploma or less (CLS).

The fathers of female deans are better educated than are the fathers of the deans as a group, with 62.6 percent having a high school diploma or less; similarly, 63.7 percent of the fathers of Hispanic deans have a high school diploma or less. Almost 90 percent of the fathers of Black deans have a high school diploma or less. Nearly 63 percent of the mothers of female deans have a high school diploma or less; almost 73 percent of the mothers of Hispanic deans have a high school diploma or less; and 66.7 percent of the mothers of Black deans have a high school diploma or less (CLS).

The educational level of the parents of current deans of instruction indicates that deans, like presidents, come from blue-collar backgrounds.

## Parents' Occupations

As with the educational level of the parents of the deans of instruction, a brief look at the occupations of the parents of presidents provides a point of comparison between presidents and deans.

Almost 18 percent of the fathers of presidents worked in administration and management. Included in this category are positions such as foreman, textile manager, accountant, banker, general contractor, and any number of similar positions. Among the other occupations ranking high were the following: agriculture (14 percent); manufacturing (9 percent); sales (8 percent); construction (8 percent); and service occupations (6 percent). Many other occupations were identified; they were too numerous to classify but were ones not normally requiring a college degree. Approximately 13 percent of the fathers of presidents held jobs in teaching, law, and the sciences, positions that normally require the bachelor's degree or above. The majority of the mothers of presidents were homemakers, with 60 percent of the presidents reporting that their mothers did not work outside the home. The largest category of employment outside the home for the mothers was in education, with 10 percent so occupied. Over 9 percent of the mothers were in administrative support positions such as secretary, and 3 percent were in health-related fields such as nursing (Vaughan, 1986, p. 11). The occupations of the mothers and fathers of current presidents further supported the blue-collar backgrounds of presidents.

Twelve percent of the fathers of current deans fall into the administrative-management category. As was the case with the presidents' fathers, 14 percent of the deans' fathers were in agriculture. Approximately 13 percent of the fathers of deans were engaged in fields requiring a bachelor's degree such as law and teaching, again an identical figure with the presidents. Seven percent were in sales; 7 percent in construction; 14 percent in manufacturing and mining; and over 30 percent in any number of occupations, including service occupations, all of which required less than a college degree. The occupations of the mothers of current deans fell into the following categories: 48 percent of the mothers were homemakers; 10.5 percent were in positions requiring the bachelor's degree or above, with education being the dominant category; almost 19 percent were in secretarial work or a similar field; and over 4 percent were in health-related fields, including nursing. Four percent worked in manufacturing and 8.6 percent in service occupations (Vaughan, 1989b, p. 113).

The educational levels and the occupations of the parents of current deans of instruction clearly indicate that most deans, as is true with most presidents, come from blue-collar backgrounds. If one describes the community college presidency as the "blue-collar presidency," as I did in my work on the subject, then one can also describe the community college's dean of instruction position as the "blue-collar deanship."

The majority of the deans, as is true with presidents, have far exceeded the educational level of their parents; moreover, they have left their blue-collar backgrounds in their past in terms of their occupational and educational achievements as well.

## Significance of Family Background

What can be concluded regarding family background other than that most deans have left their blue-collar childhood behind? In *The Community College Presidency* (Vaughan, 1986) I presented some tentative hypotheses regarding the family background of presidents. One is as follows:

> One can conclude that most of today's presidents were somehow able to extricate themselves from the great mass of people associated with the community college, including those who were interested in assuming positions of leadership, and acquire the top leadership posts themselves. In addition, these presidents could be viewed as the leading edge of a new generation freed from the Depression and World War II and catapulted to high office by rapid social, economic, and political events (p. 12).

• • •

I also concluded that family background might help to explain the missionary zeal exhibited by many community college presidents; that it might explain some of the defensiveness exhibited by presidents when the community college is criticized; and, that family background (primarily blue-collar) might help to explain the president's willingness to embrace the community college's comprehensive mission, especially occupational-technical education (Vaughan, 1986, pp. 12–14). The conclusions were based upon literature on the community college and on my own interpretations, not on interviews with presidents regarding family background.

During the interviews conducted with deans of instruction, I pointed out to them that most deans come from blue-collar backgrounds. I then asked them what effect, if any, having the majority of the deans with blue-collar backgrounds might have on the deanship and on the community college. As one might guess, there were advantages and disadvantages associated with the family backgrounds of current deans of instruction.

## Advantages of Family Background

Almost without exception, the deans believe that their blue-collar backgrounds aided them in understanding community college students, many of whom come from backgrounds similar to those of the deans. A sort of "my kind of people" mystique seemed to surround the students, as I learned from interviews with a number of the deans. One dean, for example, suggests that many community college students have a work ethic which causes them to be upwardly mobile, with the community college viewed as the vehicle for the mobility. Along the same lines, another dean believes that family background causes deans to be dedicated to their own college and to the community college in general. Speaking of deans, she notes that "probably they've seen education as something important in their lives and, in fact, as something that brought them up, improved their status. Therefore, they are convinced that the work they engage in can make the American dream come true for students." Another dean, who identified his own background as blue collar, feels that he readily identifies with the students who come to the community college: "I think I'm sensitive to their needs." The same dean feels that he wants to pass on to students what he has learned about the value of education because most students from blue-collar families do not realize its importance. A female dean at a two-year technical institute whose background is largely in technical education believes that her blue-collar background gives her a greater appreciation for students in the technical programs at her college. She remarks: "Having come from that type [blue collar] of family situation, maybe I realize the importance and value of technical positions more than those coming from stronger academic backgrounds." Another dean believes that having a blue-collar background is an advantage for community college deans. He explains:

> [The blue-collar background] allows the deans to have a good feeling about what the community college student needs—understand the type of background the students come from—and to have a greater sense of empathy for the students—an understanding of what they are going through. Personally, I'm from a blue-collar background. I'm the first member of my family to have ever gotten a college degree, and I've got brothers and sisters—there are five of us—and one brother and sister, younger, didn't even graduate from high school. Coming from that background, most of us had to work our way through college, and I see that as a strength in that we work with many students from the same background.

•••

A female dean from a blue-collar home believes that "we probably feel strongly about the mission of the community college because education helped us. I think a blue-collar background makes it a fairly pragmatic kind of approach, if nothing else. For me it makes me fairly student-oriented and interested in advocating for students and making opportunities for student success, for people who are coming from the same background that I came from."

Another dean who "was very, very lucky" in being able to attend a liberal arts college and graduate school and participate in two postdoctoral programs in Europe, credits working in the community college with inculcating in him an appreciation for students who were less fortunate than he. The blue-collar nature of the student body "made me a believer in and a fighter for the community college. I think it made me appreciate that you can work with your hands and have honor; you can be a two-year nurse and have honor... You can go here [the community college] and then go to the university after you have matured and act honorably. I think it's those values that that background gave me. And it makes me a good spokesman for the community college."

Another dean acknowledges that his own blue-collar background influenced his attitude toward the community college: "I clearly see that the community college is serving so many people, young people of the same background that I had, and I can see what the community college can do under a dean's or president's or faculty's leadership. I think from that standpoint, my background has assisted me. My background was certainly blue collar and that's the same background I see in my students in all of the institutions I've been in."

One female dean who had been at her college over 10 years but had only been a dean for one year at the time of the interview sees her blue-collar background as an asset in her current role: "I think that the more acquainted you are with a variety of perspectives, the better you do the job. So if you come from a background that matches that of many of your students, you'll understand more directly their goals and difficulties. We have so many students who are first-timers at any college, and to understand that is important rather than coming from a background where everybody's been to college and takes it for granted. I think the blue-collar background is helpful."

## Disadvantages of Family Background

As anyone from a blue-collar background can attest to, there are some disadvantages inherent in that background. Deans of instruction pointed out some of the disadvantages as they relate to the dean's position, although a number of deans interviewed saw no disadvantages, and a number felt that whatever disadvantages had existed at first had been overcome through their own education and association with other educated individuals.

One dean finds himself "in situations I did not experience as I was growing up; that is, the kinds of expectations that you would find in a dean's position—social events, cocktail hours, and those kinds of things; that's just something I've had to learn; they just didn't come with my upbringing." The same dean feels that perhaps he and those with similar backgrounds had to overcome an inferiority complex, but as the community college has matured so has the dean's position and those in it. "I think sometimes we apologize for our backgrounds a little bit. But I think we've overcome that quite a bit in the past 10 years. We have established a place for the community college, and we're proud of what we have done, what we are doing," he said. One dean, who seemed pleased with his own role and himself, believes that family background causes some deans some discomfort in their inability "to move up and down the full spectrum of the social scale as a result of family background." He goes on to note that one result may be that some deans do not feel comfortable moving into some circles within society because of their background and that "they're not going to move confidently and competently in those circles." And one dean believes that since so many of his colleagues came from blue-collar homes, the deanship loses some diversity and perceptions that "might be a healthy mixture." Another dean feels that the community college still acts as if it is "a kind of step-child of the universities and four-year colleges; we don't garner the respect that we see employees of those types of institutions having. We're still struggling to make it, in a sense, which may be part of the blue-collar background." She suggests that some community colleges continue to suffer from an inferiority complex, especially those institutions without transfer programs.

From a dean who came through the ranks from faculty member, to division chair, to dean of instruction, to academic vice-president, and who was to assume a presidency 10 days from the date of the interview, comes the following observations regarding the question on the "blue-collar deanship."

> I haven't really thought about that. That's interesting; community colleges have a little less structure, a little more focusing on the old-boy network, a little less attention paid to research. [The blue-collar background] may well have influenced the nature of community college

*leadership particularly in the late Sixties and early Seventies, although I think that's changing. [Still] I think when we enter into the collegiate environment—there's always a bit of elitism associated with that, a taint of elitism—and I think the blue-collar background probably has influenced that to a certain degree. There is some paranoia, some discomfort, because of that elitism at the higher levels of sophistication that one assumes is present at the collegiate level.*

• • •

A female dean who has been in her position for 14 years recalls her own background:

*When I was in high school, and this is the God's truth, there was a librarian who was a real model for me, and a really important woman. She took a bunch of us who were in high school who didn't know our left hand from our right, and sat us down and said, "Now this is a knife and this is a fork, and this is how you cut your meat." Along the line there were some people like that who did some things for me. My father said to me early on that it's important to be able to mix with people. Being able to talk to people, I think, is kind of significant. I'm just brash enough that my blue-collar background didn't bother me too much after I became a dean.*

• • •

As suggested in *The Community College Presidency* (Vaughan, 1986), the significance of family background on one's personal performance is difficult to determine. Nevertheless, if one is to understand current deans of instruction and their roles as current and future community college leaders, one way of looking at where the community college is going is to look at where its current academic leaders came from.

## MOBILITY

Community colleges tend to be provincial in their outlook. Whether this is an asset or liability has been debated by their defenders and critics for a number of years. The purpose of this study is not to debate the merits or shortcomings of the provincial nature of the community college. Rather, by looking at the background of presidents and deans of instruction one can understand why community colleges might be considered by some to be provincial in their outlook.

## High School Graduation

In order to determine whether the leadership of community colleges might contribute to its provincialism, both current presidents and deans were asked if they were employed in the state in which they finished high school. Forty-five percent of the current presidents were so employed, which means that almost one-half of the community colleges in the nation are led by individuals who grew up in the region served by the college (Vaughan, 1986, p. 15–16). Deans of instruction are even more likely to work within the state in which they finished high school than are presidents, with 49.4 percent of the deans currently holding positions in the state in which they grew up. Female deans are less likely to be deans in the state in which they finished high school (40 percent as reported on the CLS survey and 37 percent as reported on the Women's Survey discussed in Part II) than are male deans (52 percent); Black deans are much more likely to remain in the state in which they finished high school (63 percent) than are either presidents or the deans as a group; 54 percent of the Hispanic deans live in the state in which they finished high school (Vaughan, 1989b, p. 114).

Does it matter where a dean or president finished high school? If a purpose of the community college is to bring about changes in attitudes among the people it serves, the fact that a large number of deans and presidents come from the region served by the college might tend to perpetuate existing customs and mores. On the other hand, family background and geographic origin might well be what is needed in order to lead a community college to achieve its full potential in a specific region. Certainly one cannot or should not generalize about what an individual will do in a given situation; nevertheless, if a purpose of the community college is to bring about changes in attitudes, governing boards might want to consider the wisdom of employing presidents and deans from the college's service region. It would seem risky for a college to employ both a dean and a president from the area served by the college, for to do so is to run the risk of maintaining the status quo and losing the perspective that may result from employing at least one of the institution's two top leaders from outside the region.

## Tenure in Current Position

Current deans of instruction on the average have been in their current positions for 5.4 years, with women, Blacks, and Hispanics being in the dean's position for less time than white males (CLS). In contrast, the average tenure of presidents in their current position is 7.2 years; noteworthy, however, is that over 50 percent of the current presidents have been in their current position for five years or less (Vaughan, 1986, p. 210). Almost 68 percent of the current deans of instruction state that they are very likely or somewhat likely to move to a new position within the next five years (CLS). Advice often given to aspiring presidents is: be willing to change positions by moving to a new college, a new city, a new state. Those deans aspiring to the presidency tend to be more willing to move than those deans who do not have the presidency as a career goal.

## EDUCATIONAL BACKGROUND

Almost 70 percent of the current deans hold the doctorate. Of those, almost 33 percent hold the Ph.D., and 36 percent hold the Ed.D.; 25 percent of the current deans hold the master's degree (Vaughan, 1989b, pp. 117–118). The 70 percent of deans with the doctorate compares with 75 percent of the presidents with the doctorate. Thirty-two percent of the presidents have the Ph.D., and 44 percent have the Ed.D. (Vaughan, 1986, p. 19). In the case of both deans and presidents, those possessing the Ph.D. may have the degree in education, including higher education. For example, 54 percent of the deans holding the Ph.D. majored in education with 41 percent of them majoring in higher education (CLS). In any event, if one is seeking major differences between the educational background of deans and presidents, they are likely to be disappointed, for the educational backgrounds are indeed similar.

## PROFESSIONAL MEMBERSHIPS

Membership in professional associations may give some indication of where individuals place their professional loyalties. Deans of instruction were asked to list the professional organizations to which they belong, excluding institutional memberships, such as the AACJC.

Over 80 percent of the deans responding to the survey question regarding professional membership stated that they belong to one or more professional associations. It should be noted, however, that of the 619 deans responding to the survey, 118 (19 percent) did not respond to the question on professional membership. The most popular organization listed by the deans responding to the survey was the American Association of Higher Education (AAHE), with 34 percent (207 deans) stating that they are members (Vaughan, 1989b, p. 118). Interestingly, of the approximately 70 percent of the current presidents who responded to the question regarding professional membership on the presidential survey (181 of the 591 presidents did not respond to this question), 53 percent (218 presidents) stated that they belong to the AAHE (Vaughan, 1986, p. 214).

In one report of its membership, the AAHE (Edgerton, 1989) noted that chief academic officers and deans comprise the largest category of membership with nearly 1,800 of the 6,500 members coming from those groups. By grouping deans and chief academic officers into one category, it is impossible to determine how many of the members of AAHE are chief academic officers. The same source noted that more than 900 of its members are presidents of four- and two-year institutions. In any event, the nation's community colleges are well represented in the AAHE, thereby providing a potentially important forum for community college leaders, and one that is not used as often or as well as it could be.

The next most popular organization among deans is the Phi Delta Kappa (PDK), with almost 28 percent of the deans who responded to the question regarding professional membership holding membership in that organization (Vaughan, 1989b, p. 118). The PDK was the most popular organization among presidents, with 62 percent of those responding to the question on professional membership stating that they belong to it (Vaughan, 1986, p. 214). Other professional organizations to which deans belong are the National Association of College and University Business Officers (almost 9 percent belong), although the percent belonging might be misleading since this organization offers institutional membership that is likely paid for by the institution; the Association for the Study of Higher Education (6 percent); the American Educational Research Association (over 3 percent); and the American College Personnel Association (3 percent). Forty-six percent of the deans responding to the survey mentioned various other professional associations to which they belong, many of which are based in their discipline or teaching field (Vaughan, 1989b, pp. 118–119).

Professional memberships help to interpret the roles of deans and presidents. For example, the large percentage of presidents (over 30 percent) and deans (19 percent) who listed no professional memberships would seem to be high for members of a profession that depends upon the distribution, interpretation, and advancement of knowledge—key roles played by professional associations.

Professional memberships also may be an extension of the position one occupies. For example, I suggested earlier that organizations such as the locally based PDK provide presidents with excellent political (in the broader sense of the term) and social contacts, as well as professional ones. Perhaps these contacts are not seen as being as important to the deanship as they are to the presidency. I also suggested that presidents may tend to be more active (in terms of attending national meetings) in some professional associations than deans simply because when presidents travel, someone must stay at home and mind the store, a task often performed by the dean of instruction (Vaughan, 1989b, p. 119).

## PUBLICATIONS AND RESEARCH

Forty-nine percent of the deans responding to the survey stated that they had done research within the last five years; 38 percent stated that they had published something within the past five years. Women are more likely to have done research or published something within the last five years than their male counterparts, while Hispanics are more likely and Blacks are slightly less likely to have done research and published something during the same time period than the deans as a whole (CLS and Vaughan, 1989b, pp. 119–120). In contrast to the deans, 39 percent of the presidents stated that they had engaged in research in the past four years, and 36 percent stated that they had published something within the same four-year period (Vaughan, 1986, p. 216).

Should the chief academic officer of a community college engage in research and produce publications? One would think that if any administrator on campus should engage in such activities, it should be the academic dean. On the other hand, the community college has not emphasized research and publications, and the dean who devotes an inordinate amount of time to these activities might face some resistance within the institution. Perhaps rather than engaging in research in the traditional sense of the term, deans should devote more time and energy to the broader aspects of scholarship. More will be said on this subject later.

## DEANS' WORKLOAD

The workload of any professional person is difficult to determine. For example, is the evening meeting of the service club or professional organization a part of the workload? Certainly, if a dean is expected to represent the college in an organization, then attending meetings of the organization would be a part of the workload, regardless of when the organization meets. On the other hand, if one belongs to an organization for one's own enjoyment and self-fulfillment, then attendance at meetings is hardly part of the workload. In any event, the deans were asked how many hours a week they work.

Deans of instruction work an average of 51 hours a week, with little difference between sexes (females work 51.4 hours per week) or ethnic or racial minorities. Those deans aspiring to the presidency do not work longer hours than those who do not have presidential aspirations (CLS), thus suggesting that there may be an optimal number of hours required in the dean's position, regardless of one's career plans. (This is not meant to imply that deans with presidential ambitions would be expected to work longer hours than other deans, although some individuals relate career ambitions to hours worked.)

Deans must enjoy their work, for although they earn an average of 20 days of vacation each year, on average they take only 13 days (Vaughan, 1989b, p. 123). Deans' use of vacation time mirrors that of presidents, who earn an average of 21 days of vacation annually and take 13 days (Vaughan, 1986, p. 213). One can speculate that presidents set the vacation pattern and deans follow the pattern. Or, maybe deans, as is true with professionals in many fields, just like to keep some vacation days "in the bank." And there is always the possibility that the dean's position is perceived by those occupying the position to be so demanding that vacation time must be limited.

## THE DEANS' CHIEF CONFIDANT

The professional relationship between the dean of instruction and the president of an institution often is close, with each needing someone in whom to confide. Presidents especially suffer from the "lonely at the top" syndrome. To whom do presidents and deans turn when they need someone in whom to confide?

Over 27 percent of community college presidents named the institution's chief academic officer as their chief confidant. The 27 percent contrasts sharply with the 2.7 percent of the presidents who named the institution's chief student services officer as their chief confidant (Vaughan, 1986, p. 39). Does the president-dean confidant relationship hold from the dean's perspective?

Two-hundred and twenty-two (33 percent) of the deans responding to the survey named the president of the institution as their chief confidant. The next largest group (24 percent) of confidants is made up of other deans, including deans of instruction, deans of student services, and deans of financial services. Other confidants are associate deans, spouses (3.43 percent of the respondents listed their spouse), chancellors, division chairs, and various other individuals on campus (CLS).

Based upon the number of deans and presidents who share each other's confidence, one can readily conclude what most presidents and deans have always known: the relationship between the president and dean of instruction is extremely important to those occupying the positions, and that relationship requires mutual trust and respect.

## THE DEAN AT HOME

The deanship, as is true of the presidency, does not exist in a vacuum. Deans marry, have children, participate in recreational activities, and have friends. The following is a brief look at some of the more personal aspects of the lives of those individuals who currently serve as deans of instruction in the nation's community colleges.

### Marital Status

Of those deans responding to the CLS survey, over 87 percent are married, over 6 percent are divorced, 5.6 percent are single, and 1.2 percent are widowed. Sixty-three percent of the female deans are married, according to the CLS (65 percent of those responding to the Women's Survey reported that they are married) and 19 percent are divorced, implying that, for whatever reasons, it may be more difficult for women to maintain both a high-level professional position and a marriage than it is for men.

The marital status of deans varies somewhat from that of presidents. Ninety-two percent of the presidents reported that they are married, with only 2 percent reporting that they are single (Vaughan, 1986, p. 20). The difference may suggest that some presidents stay married in order to promote the image of the happy family, an image that is seen as an asset in some presidential positions, while the less visible dean may not feel the need to project the family image. Also, only about 6 percent of the current presidents are women, whereas 21 percent of the current deans are women; therefore, the larger number of women deans coupled with the larger percentage of women who are divorced or single would increase the percentage of unmarried deans. In any event, the marriage profile of the deans as a whole does not vary greatly from that of the presidents as a whole.

### The Dean's Spouse

The average age of the dean's spouse is approximately 46, two years younger than the average age of deans. Almost eight out of 10 spouses of deans work in paid occupations outside the home, whereas over six out of 10 spouses of presidents work for pay outside the home (Vaughan, 1989b, p. 122). As more and more of the current deans assume the presidency, the idea of getting two for one (historically, the female spouse came "free") when the president is employed becomes less likely for those governing boards and institutions that cling to the idea of a spouse who devotes large amounts of time in the service of the college coming along as part of the presidential package. Also, as more and more women become presidents, the chances that their spouses will function exclusively as homemakers decreases. Working spouses have neither the time, energy, nor inclination to do any great amount of entertaining, especially if they are expected to do more than just be there. The faculty wives' clubs and similar organizations have all but disappeared from the scene (Vaughan, 1986, pp. 153–154). One must wonder if entertaining in the home, with the spouse hosting the event, can be far behind (even if there were not inherent legal risks), especially if the spouse is supposed to prepare the food.

Eighty-six percent of the spouses of deans have at least a high school diploma, compared to 80 percent of the spouses of presidents. Of those, over 51 percent of the spouses of deans have the bachelor's degree, with 31 percent holding the master's degree; close to 9 percent have the doctor's degree; and almost 29 percent received an associate degree from a community college (CLS).

While there are some differences between the spouses of deans and the spouses of presidents, the differences are in degree rather than kind. Indeed, those deans who assume the presidency will have spouses who are, for the most part, very similar to the spouses of current presidents, with the likely expectation that more spouses will be males in the future.

### Friends and Acquaintances

As shown by the educational levels of the parents of current deans, most come from blue-collar backgrounds. Indeed, the great majority of deans are first-generation college students. Most deans have far exceeded the educational level and professional accomplishments of their parents. One result of moving up the economic and social scale is that it is very difficult to maintain friendships from one's childhood. In addition, the mobility of deans removes many of them from the environment of their childhood. Not surprisingly, both deans and spouses of deans have left their childhood friends in the past, with only 5 percent of the deans and 8 percent of the spouses stating that they spend at least 30 minutes a week with childhood friends. Whom, then, do deans and their spouses see socially for at least 30 minutes a week?

Not surprisingly, deans spend more time with their colleagues than with any other single group, with 77 percent stating that they spend more than 30 minutes a week in social situations with their colleagues. Over 50 percent of the spouses also spend more than 30 minutes a week socializing with colleagues. The next most important social group for both deans (52 percent) and spouses (61 percent) are neighbors. Friends from church compose important social contacts for both spouses and deans, with 46 percent of both stating that they spend 30 minutes or more each week with friends from church. Other important social contacts for both deans and spouses are club associates and other friends (CLS).

## Club Memberships and Leisure-Time Activities

Sixty-eight percent of all deans and 56 percent of the female deans responding to the survey stated that they belong to one or more civic or fraternal organizations. The most popular service club for deans is the Rotary, with 26 percent stating that they are members (65 percent of the presidents belonging to a service club state that they belong to the Rotary). Other popular service clubs to which deans belong are the Kiwanis (11 percent), the Lions (8 percent), and the fraternal organization, the Masons (5 percent). Almost 16 percent of the Blacks list membership in the Masons (CLS). In no case does the percentage of deans holding membership in a civic or fraternal organization exceed that of presidents.

One conclusion reached by this writer earlier was that a smaller percentage of deans join service clubs than do presidents because presidents, more so than deans, use service club membership as an extension of the president's office (Vaughan, 1989b, p. 121). The percentage of deans who are women versus the percentage of presidents who are women also would influence service club membership, since most service clubs to which presidents and deans belong in large numbers, and especially the popular Rotary and Kiwanis clubs, are male-dominated and in some cases exclusively male.[1]

---

[1] In order to decide what service clubs to include on the original CLS sent to presidents, a small poll of club membership among presidents was taken. The clubs listed on the presidential CLS survey included those that were identified by the poll, as did the CLS survey sent to the deans of instruction. Both surveys had an "other" category for listing organizations not included on the survey. The "other" category, however, did not prevent some female deans from criticizing this section of the survey. One female dean wrote me a rather lengthy and harsh letter explaining that she refused to complete my sexist survey. Seventeen female deans responding to the survey wrote comments on the survey indicating their displeasure with the clubs and organizations listed. One of those comments, "Why *boys'* groups?," should serve as a reminder to men (including this author) to be sensitive to asking questions on surveys that could be interpreted as sexist. Another simply said: "Yuk! All male bastions." Ironically, no female president responding to the original CLS survey

## Fun and Games

In general, deans and presidents engage in similar leisure-time activities, such as golf, jogging, tennis, swimming, skiing, fishing, hunting, and any number of activities pursued by many Americans (Vaughan, 1986, pp. 23–24; Vaughan, 1989b, p. 122). Jogging tops the list of physical activities engaged in by deans of instruction (90 percent of the deans engage in one or more sports), with 30 percent of the deans who answered the survey listing jogging as one of their physical activities, whereas 31 percent of the presidents jog. In contrast, the top sport for presidents is golf, with 39 percent stating that they play golf, whereas 23 percent of the deans play golf. Often golf and country club membership go hand in hand. Sixteen percent of the deans are members of a country club (12 percent of the women deans are members), and 54 percent who belong to a country club use it for professional entertaining (CLS). In contrast, 32 percent of the presidents belong to a country club, and 80 percent of those who belong use it for professional entertaining (Vaughan, 1986, pp. 23–24). Playing golf and holding country club membership may, even in today's society, indicate that the community college professional has "made it," and while speculations are always somewhat suspect, influences regarding the percentage of deans who play golf versus the percentage of presidents who play may aid in understanding some subtle differences between the positions: presidents may well use golf and country club membership as a means of making contacts and "deals" that are viewed as beneficial to the institution (Vaughan, 1989b, p. 122); it may be easier for a larger percentage of presidents to get away from the office during "golfing hours" than it is for deans, especially if the dean is in charge when the president is away at play; country club membership is part of the benefits package offered to some presidents, if not implying that presidents should play golf, certainly making it easier for them to do so; and, as suggested above, presidents have more control over their agenda, more escape hatches, than do deans, thereby being able to engage

---

criticized the service club membership section. Perhaps once one makes it to the presidency, service club membership is placed in a broader perspective. On the other hand, the larger number of deans and the percentage of female deans versus female presidents responding to the survey increased the chances of criticism. In any event, service club membership remains a point of contention for some community college professionals. For example, one president of a medium-sized community college in the South noted that "Membership in the Rotary Club comes with the presidency in this area" (Vaughan, 1989b, p. 121). A female president, when asked if there were any advantages in relationship to the presidency resulting from her sex replied: "Yes, I don't have to join the Rotary Club!" (Vaughan, 1989b, p. 86). In any event, should I ever again ask a question regarding service club membership, I will be more sensitive and will include clubs to which women traditionally belong, including all-female clubs.

in off-campus activities on a regular and irregular basis more easily than deans.

## SUMMARY

In order to draw a composite profile of the community college dean of instruction, I surveyed the chief academic officers of the nation's public community, technical, and junior colleges using an instrument almost identical to the questionnaire employed in my 1985 survey of community college presidents. Major findings from the dean's survey include the following:

- Chief academic officers and presidents have similar family and educational backgrounds. Most grew up in blue-collar environments and have far exceeded the educational levels attained by their parents. While the majority of the deans and presidents hold doctorates (70 and 75 percent, respectively), 75 to 80 percent report that their parents attained no higher credential than the high school diploma. Interviews with the deans confirm that their blue-collar roots led them to empathize with community college students who are (on average) likely to have similar backgrounds and see the college as a vehicle for upward mobility.

- Almost half of the presidents and deans of instruction (45 and 49 percent, respectively) held positions in the states in which they grew up. While there may be advantages to filling leadership positions with professionals from the local community, this practice may have the untoward effect of perpetuating the community college's provincial outlook.

- Approximately 80 percent of the deans belong to professional associations, compared to 70 percent of the presidents. When asked to name the professional associations they belong to, the American Association of Higher Education (AAHE) was most often cited by the deans, along with a wide range of organizations that are based on the deans' teaching fields. It is discouraging to note, however, the surprisingly large proportion of both presidents and deans (30 and 20 percent, respectively) who listed no professional memberships.

- On average, deans work 51 hours per week and, like the presidents, rarely use all of their vacation time. When asked to name their chief on-the-job confidant, one-third of the deans listed the president, another 25 percent listed other deans on campus, and the remainder listed a variety of other individuals, including spouses, associate deans, chancellors, and division chairs.

• Despite the fact that community colleges do not emphasize traditional research leading to publication, sizable minorities of the deans indicate that they have conducted research at some time over the past five years (49 percent) and that they have published something over the past five years (38 percent). Nonetheless, research and writing remain peripheral tasks in the deans' professional lives, which are dominated by administrative concerns.

• On the whole, the personal lives of the deans of instruction—in terms of marital status, spouses' characteristics, friends and acquaintances, club memberships, and leisure-time activities—do not vary significantly from the personal lives of the presidents. Where differences do occur, however, gender seems to play a role. The fact that deans are slightly less likely to be married and less likely to join service clubs may stem from the fact that 21 percent of the deans are women, compared to only 6 percent of the presidents. More will be said about the role of women in Chapter 4.

There is little in the findings to support the hypothesis that the next generation of presidents will differ greatly from the current generation, assuming that deans of instruction will continue to move up the ladder in the future to the same degree that they have in the past. As I concluded in *Leadership in Transition* (Vaughan, 1989b):

> The overwhelming conclusion reached here is that the next generation of community college presidents will, assuming the current deans of instruction fill their fair share of the presidencies, be a mirror image of the current generation of presidents in almost all respects. This mirror image runs the gamut from family background to family life, from academic degrees to views and practices of scholarship, from sports activities to professional memberships. Even the numbers of days of vacation taken each year by deans is a mirror image of the number of days taken by presidents.... If one accepts as fact that many of the next generation of presidents will come from the current group of deans of instruction, then indeed, the community college presidency will change little over the next decade...(p. 123)

• • •

This is not to say that the president's role will remain unchanged. Stated another way, will the current deans who assume the presidency resemble current presidents? The answer is yes. Will they approach the presidency in the same way as current presidents? The answer is "likely not," for as the presidency changes, the successful occupant of the position must also change, must have new visions, and must face new challenges, for the position molds the individual just as the individual molds the position.

# 3

# Assuming the Deanship

∎

The previous chapter presented facts, figures, and observations regarding deans of instruction in the nation's community colleges. Many of the data were personal: educational level, family background, activities away from the office, and other information that contributes to the profile of the individuals who occupy the position. The present chapter examines the pathways to the deanship, including some steps not taken, some lessons not learned.

## MOVING THROUGH THE ADMINISTRATIVE RANKS

The dean of instruction's position is so interrelated with the community college president's position that it is difficult to discuss the pathway to the deanship without some reference to the presidency, especially when one considers that one out of every two deans of instruction will likely become a president. With this in mind, a brief reference to the presidency helps one to understand some aspects of the pathway followed as one moves through the community college's administrative ranks.

*The Community College Presidency* (Vaughan, 1986) confirmed what many individuals associated with community colleges suspected: one can increase one's chances of becoming a community college president by moving through the academic pipeline. The typical pathway is from teacher to department head or assistant division chair, to division chair, to associate or assistant dean, to dean of instruction or academic vice-president. Of the 590 presidents responding to the question regarding their position prior to assuming their first presidency (positions preceding the deanship were not examined), over 38 percent were chief academic officers immediately prior to assuming the presidency, and over 12 percent were vice-presidents, a position that normally oversees the instructional program (Vaughan, 1986, pp. 27–28). Thus, using the terminology of this current volume, over 50 percent of the current presidents were deans of instruction immediately prior to assuming their first presidency. Of course, presidents came from practically every source imaginable; nevertheless, one can increase the odds of becoming a community college president by moving through academic positions, for the pathway most traveled on the way to the president's office is the one leading directly from the dean of instruction's office.

One of the reasons many individuals want to become a dean of instruction is that the position is the major jumping-off point for the presidency. Once individuals reach the dean of instruction's position, they realize they have reached a plateau in their career that is "only a heartbeat away" from the presidency; they also know the pathway they followed in reaching the deanship. On the other hand, for those individuals who want to move through the administrative ranks but have not yet reached the dean's position, the most immediate question becomes not "How does one become a president?" but rather, "How does one become a dean of instruction?"

## PATHWAYS TO THE DEANSHIP

The most important single source of deans of instruction is the division chair's position, with over 29 percent occupying the chair's position immediately prior to assuming their first dean of instruction position. Another 11 percent were either associate or assistant deans of instruction prior to becoming a dean, thus clearly establishing the traditional academic pipeline as the most important avenue to the deanship (CLS). Although the division chair's position is the most important single pathway to the deanship, it is by no means the only one. Even by adding to the total the 11 percent who were associate or assistant deans, the 40 percent moving into the dean's position through the traditional pathway is below the more than 50 percent of the presidents who were their institution's chief academic officer prior to assuming the presidency. One can conclude that the roadway that deans of instruction travel is relatively broad but becomes a narrow pathway once one assumes the deanship and aspires to the presidency.

Nine percent of the deans of instruction were deans of student services (the title varies) immediately prior to assuming the dean of instruction's position. A number of talented deans of student services with whom I have talked over the years indicated that they felt they would have to move into the instructional pipeline if they were to achieve the presidency, thus, in part, accounting for the 9 percent who chose to switch rather than fight. A dean of student services expressed his views on the pathway to the presidency with a pithy comment: "I know what it is not; it is not through the dean of student services" (quoted in Vaughan, 1986, p. 39). While one dean's comments do not make the case for switching positions if one wants to be a president, the aspiring president should not ignore that 7.8 percent of the current presidents were deans of student services prior to assuming the presidency whereas, as noted above, almost 50 percent of the current presidents were their institution's chief academic officer prior to assuming the presidency (Vaughan, 1986, pp. 27–29).

Even if one does not have the presidency as a career goal, there are other reasons why a dean of student services might want to switch to the dean of instruction's position. For example, on most campuses an Orwellian pecking order exists whereby all of the deans are equal on the organizational chart, yet one dean, the dean of instruction, is more equal than the others. Faculty members, presidents, and board members tend to favor deans of instruction when seeking a leader. The dean of instruction is often in charge when the president is off campus; 25 percent (137) of the presidents pointed to the dean of instruction as their chief confidant, whereas 2.7 percent (16) of the presidents named the dean of student services as their chief confidant (Vaughan, 1986, p. 39). These acts are observed and noted by members of the college community and by members of the college's board, thus adding to the prestige of the dean of instruction's position while, perhaps by default, lessening the prestige associated with the dean of student services' position.

A high percentage of the deans moved into their first deanship from the position of faculty member, with over 12 percent of the current deans stating that they were faculty members prior to assuming their first deanship. The percentage of faculty members seemed large; therefore, the data were examined to see if any discernible patterns existed that set apart those deans who had moved from the faculty to the deanship from those who had followed different routes.

Fifty-six males (11.7 percent of all male deans) moved into the dean-ship directly from a faculty position, as did 18 females (14.4 percent of all female deans). The male-female mix does not indicate any pattern that would set these deans apart; the percentage and mix of male and female faculty assuming the deanship do, however, support the above sugges-tion that the base for the deanship is relatively large, whereas the path-way narrows once one moves from the dean's position to the presiden-cy, for the number of faculty members moving directly into the presidency is insignificant, although one can almost always find an exception when dealing with over 900 presidencies, and one or two presidents indicated that they had moved directly into the presidency from a faculty position (Vaughan, 1986, p. 28).

The average age of those deans who moved from a faculty position to the deanship is almost 48 years, the same as the average age of the deans as a whole. Had the deans moving from faculty positions been con-siderably older than the average age of all deans, one might conclude that they had obtained the deanship at a time when community colleges were younger and deans with administrative experience were less avail-able. The average college size in which the former faculty members serve as deans is 2,265 full-time students, thus dispelling any belief that they assumed the deanship at only small colleges. What can one conclude? Probably that the faculty members were well respected by members of the college community and were in the right place at the right time, con-clusions one can make about most positions.

Over 9 percent of the deans of instruction were deans or directors of community services and continuing education (the title varies) prior to assuming the dean of instruction's position. While this category should perhaps be grouped with positions of academic leadership, and therefore should be considered as a part of the academic pipeline (equal to divi-sion chair, or in some cases equal to the dean of instruction's position in terms of preparation for the presidency), community services and con-tinuing education positions vary so much from state to state and even from campus to campus within a state that a separate category seems warranted for this study. Nevertheless, previously I argued that the dean of community services' position should be considered as an important training ground for the presidency, for individuals in these positions man-age budgets; plan programs; employ and work with large numbers of faculty, many of whom teach part time; meet with diverse constituents, including leaders of business and industry and local political leaders; and perform any number of the tasks required in the presidency (Vaughan, 1987, pp. 3–10). As a matter of fact, 4.6 percent of the current presidents were deans of community services immediately prior to assuming the presidency (Vaughan, 1986, p. 28). More importantly for this study, the 9 percent of community services deans who moved into the dean of instruction's position make community services and continuing education important jumping-off points for assuming the dean of instruction's position, and once there, the former community services deans are in an excellent position to assume the presidency and to use the skills they learned in both deans' positions.

Almost 6 percent of the deans of instruction came from positions at four-year institutions; over 2 percent were department chairs; almost 2 percent were assistants to the president; slightly over 4 percent made lateral moves (from one dean of instruction position to another); less than 1 percent were high school administrators; and less than 1 percent were directors of evening programs.[1] The remainder came from any number of sources, including four who were former community college presidents, a hospital administrator, a director of guidance, an executive director of the state-level commission for community colleges, an associate director of an accrediting agency, three directors of admissions, and from any number of other positions, including one who stated that the position occupied prior to becoming a dean was that of student.

One conclusion regarding the pathway to the deanship is that it is far from straight and narrow but rather has many branches. Nevertheless, the most traveled pathway is the one leading through the academic forest, with the division chair's position as the jumping-off point most likely to land one in the dean of instruction's position.

## PREPARATION FOR THE DEANSHIP

Deans of instruction rarely experienced the "shock waves" upon assuming their first deanship often felt by presidents assuming their first presidency. Indeed, none of the deans interviewed felt intimidated upon

---

[1] The myth persists in some circles that community colleges still turn to public schools and four-year institutions for their deans and presidents. The myth did not develop without some basis. For example, in 1960 over 24 percent of the community college presidents came from positions in public school administration, and over 15 percent came from positions at four-year institutions. By 1986, over 90 percent of the presidents came from community college ranks. The small percentage of deans coming from public schools and four-year institutions further indicates that it is time to put the myth to rest: the community college does not now and probably will not in the future turn to public schools or four-year institutions for its top leaders. See *The Community College Presidency* (Vaughan, 1986, pp. 28–29; 40) for a discussion of the decline in the number of presidents coming from the public school and four-year institution's ranks.

assuming the deanship. To the contrary, most deans felt that their educational background and experience prepared them well for most aspects of the position. Nevertheless, most deans felt that there were certain gaps in their experience and background and, as is true with most positions, that they had a number of things to learn about the position once they became deans.

One of the most important differences most deans discovered upon moving into the position was that in order to be successful deans of instruction, they had to view the college from a much broader perspective than was the case when they were division chairs or in similar positions with narrower scopes and more limited responsibilities than the dean's position. For example, just the seemingly obvious task of keeping up with the literature in higher education became more important for one individual who moved from the division chair's position into the deanship. He notes: "Even though I had a doctorate in higher education administration, I really did not spend as much time as I should on the literature of higher education while a division chair. That hurt me some, required me to catch up when I became a dean." Another dean of instruction explains his reaction to his expanded responsibilities as follows:

> As a division director, I was a full-time administrator responsible for a smaller area—math, science, and health occupations. By moving to the dean's level, my responsibilities were obviously broader and more encompassing. [As dean] I certainly was comfortable working with the faculty in those three areas and was able to work with them closely; when they spoke about needs I had an understanding of what those needs were. It is much more difficult in the social sciences, the humanities, or developmental education. That's not my background; it's not my experience. So, being able to interpret the kinds of things I was hearing from faculty was difficult.

• • •

One current dean who had been at her college for 10 years prior to becoming dean of instruction and who felt generally well prepared for assuming the deanship (she had been both an assistant and an associate dean) found that in order to survive, she had to master the budget quickly, which, with the help of her staff, she did. She is now looking at what skills and experiences she will need should she take the next step (the presidency) in the administrative hierarchy, a step she feels she will likely take in the not-too-distant future.

Another dean who came to the deanship from the dean of student services' position found no surprises when he moved to the instructional side of the house, although he found that working with the faculty "and trying to provide leadership for them was a challenge, but I don't think there were any surprises."

## Voids in Preparation

While there were not many surprises awaiting deans upon assuming the deanship, a number discovered voids in their background that had to be filled once they assumed the position. One dean noted the following:

*Oh, I think the void—and I think it's probably common in a lot of deans—is that we tend to come from academic backgrounds. We don't come from backgrounds that emphasize leadership and management. That whole area, and there's a whole world out there, most of us learn it by the seat of our pants. We take a course here, we take a course there, we read, but really, we have no formal training in leadership and management. I think that's a real void.*

• • •

Another dean echoes a similar theme regarding the lack of leadership training prior to assuming the deanship. Some of the strengths he brought to the position were more narrowly focused than might be desirable. He notes the following, for example:

*I was trained in the discipline of biology and had attended a very good program that focused very strongly on the teaching-learning process. But I had absolutely no training or exposure to leadership responsibilities. Even some of the simple techniques and tricks in terms of how to motivate people, how to direct a relatively challenging group of faculty to come to some kind of conclusion, simple reading of financial statements, making reports, coalescing data for accreditation documents,—all that information which is fundamental to the kinds of roles that one has as a chairperson and as a dean—were not there.*

• • •

The void in leadership training prevented one dean from solving a difficult organizational problem early in his career. He believes had he had more time and more training in providing leadership, he could have been more effective in solving the problem.

In contrast to the above statement regarding coming from an academic background, one dean discovered that the lack of a traditional academic background presented him with some problems upon assuming the deanship. He describes his situation as follows:

> *Yes, I have found that I have some voids. I guess the greatest void in my educational background was that I taught in public schools and went into public school administration and from there into college administration in continuing education. So my degrees are in education; my master's, for instance, is in public school administration, and my doctorate in higher education administration. The void: I would rather have a master's degree in a discipline area.*

• • •

The dean noted, however, that he had not experienced a credibility gap with the faculty as a result of his educational background. Nevertheless, he felt that a master's degree in a discipline would enhance his performance as a dean.

A dean whose academic discipline was art history discovered that, although she had been the chair of a large division, she was not familiar with vocational programs and how they are funded. She also discovered the need to understand state financing more than was the case as division chair, but most importantly she had not "previously had the opportunity to be in closed sessions with the board." Meeting in closed sessions was an eye-opener for her, and she says she can now "really appreciate the relationship between the board and the president."

A dean who had been in her position for nine months notes that dealing with the budget and other financial matters presented her with a major problem and "the one I'm feeling most." She also had difficulty in planning how to use personnel in the service of the entire institution. Another dean, in spite of 19 years of administrative experience (two academic deanships and tenure as a dean of admissions) still discovered a void he had to fill upon assuming his current deanship: the ability to listen to what people have to say, "to really hear them, not just have them talk, for what they have to say is important and adds to the picture something I might not have thought of." Another dean, alluding to a lack of time to do everything, found that his previous position of division chair had not taught him to delegate tasks as well as he should, a skill he had to learn as dean in order to survive.

## ASSUMING THE OFFICE

How do deans of instruction view the position once they assume the deanship? What are the major rewards associated with the position? Frustrations?

### Rewards

The greatest reward of the office for a number of deans comes from seeing students achieve their goals. One response: "Well, last week was commencement. Watching the students that I've helped was rewarding. I may not be helping them individually, I may never see them, but knowing that because I worked with the faculty to create a new program, to get funding for something, or secured other resources, whether computers or books or whatever it took to get the services for students, that's the reward." From another dean: "I guess I'd say my major rewards are usually the student outcomes. When we see our students go through our system, being able to compete with any other institution academically and succeed, that is rewarding." He continues: "Education is a people endeavor. I enjoy being with people, and I enjoy being a part of it. I think when any of us succeed, the student, the rest of the staff, all of us succeed; and it's a kind of reward for me as well as for them." One veteran of three deanships confesses: "I can still get moist-eyed at some of our graduation ceremonies. Probably one of the most moving times I ever saw was when I gave a man, I believe he was 82 years old, his GED." Another veteran who has been an academic dean for 13 years points to "student success, watching students graduate, seeing students who have been successful because of a particular service or program that you've set up. I think that's perhaps the greatest reward."

Another dean, in discussing his rewards, places the deanship into a perspective that helps all administrators to understand the need to step back from the position occasionally. His analysis:

> The greatest rewards are when you back up and look at the whole thing and you see the growth opportunities that you're providing; you see students of all ages coming through those opportunities and realizing their goals and finding the fulfillment they're looking for in life—that's the greatest satisfaction of all. One has to reflect upon that as an administrator because it's somewhat further removed than the fulfillment the teacher finds in the day-to-day interaction with the student in the classroom. You don't have quite the same sense of satisfaction without sitting back and reflecting on it now and then.

• • •

Another dean gets her reward from "tremendous faculty support," support and recognition that helped her obtain the position and that has helped her gain the support of the president for the institution's instructional program. She also admits that she enjoys the prestige of the position: "I wanted this position for quite some time. To get the position, I had to wait for my predecessor to retire since I was not willing to relocate geographically. So, I waited." Another dean finds that he "certainly gets more recognition, and there's no question that can be a heady experience. I think that when your college is doing well and it is attributed to the dean's position, that feels good. Also, a lot of people depend upon you for advice and ask for your opinions, and that is important to a person's ego." Similarly, from another dean: "Taking an idea right through and then seeing a graduating class from that program, that's been very rewarding. Helping a faculty member, a new faculty member, who indicates afterwards that 'yes,' something you did made it a little more comfortable. That, those things, I think are the rewards."

One dean, while finding working with the faculty rewarding, finds working with other administrators as part of a team extremely rewarding. Especially satisfying to him is working with the president because he and the president complement each other. The same dean, reflecting upon the satisfaction he achieves from teamwork, achieved great satisfaction from his role in developing a master plan that involved the faculty and the community and is the "kind of document that doesn't collect dust on a shelf for the next seven years...I think to be able to see that kind of plan fulfilled is a great reward for me." Another dean refers to the planning role of the dean: "I think that you can identify long-range goals, and as a result of identifying these goals, you can organize the college in such a way that you can see the college move toward the goals. That's very rewarding, not only for you as an individual, but for the college as a whole."

Serving as a mentor and role model, while not mentioned specifically by a large number of deans (no specific questions were asked during the interview relating to the role of mentor or role model), was implied by many through describing their relationships with faculty and students. One dean speaks specifically of the satisfaction he gets from serving as a mentor. Indeed, one of the major satisfactions coming with the deanship is that he "really enjoys seeing an individual who is working with me develop, and for me to feel that I contributed to that—that's a real reward for me." The same dean believes that he should serve as a role model for faculty and other administrators, especially in the area of professional development. He notes:

*I encourage faculty to attend professional meetings, to be active. I've always encouraged them to publish if they've got something publishable. I try to do that through talking, letting them know I support this type of thing. One of the standing rules that I've always used as far as guiding myself is that faculty members who have a paper accepted at a meeting, we'll find the travel money for them. I've always tried to publish myself, as a model.*

• • •

One dean gets his rewards from "making things work." The following analysis of what he considers to be good about the position is revealing and offers a good snapshot of what the position might well be like on a daily basis:

*Well, if you do it right, it's a little like the rewards of the president's office, but maybe without some of the political and external hassles. We're really here for instruction. And if I pull off a new program, the finance dean and the student services dean have to agree with me. We have to do it together, and I have to get all this stuff together from the community. When I look at it, I really don't do that much work. I have somehow asked, cajoled, hopefully motivated others to do the work for me. But when it all comes together, it really is mine. I sometimes don't even get the credit for it. Often, I send a department chair who has really done the work before the board, but I know, and I think the president knows, that I pulled those things together. It's making a success of a program that really makes me feel good. I think that there's a fear or a problem with instructional deans who think they're just doing instruction. But if you are doing programming and instruction, curriculum building, and faculty development, you, as dean, have to orchestrate the whole unit. If you're doing that, you're able to do just about anything. I like managing— orchestrating the whole business—but occasionally I like to take one little pet project and enjoy doing it.*

• • •

Other comments of a similar nature were offered by a number of deans. One dean, however, reflecting on her 14 years in the position, offers a good summary of the rewards associated with the position, ranging from the vicarious rewards of graduation ceremonies and mentoring to the more personal rewards of being in the eye of the storm.

*I love working with the different subject areas. The way an English teacher approaches the problem contrasted with the way an engineer approaches it is a thing of gossamer gaiety. I mean, it really is. I love that. There's a kind of camaraderie with the president and the president's cabinet that I enjoy. I like the perks of the position. I really like that. I like being in charge. I like thinking I'm making the difference. I like setting the agenda. I like the opportunities it provides to do things like work with the National Council of Instructional Administrators, to go on the circuit and make a speech now and then. I enjoy that. Are you going to ask me the things I don't like? [I did.]*

• • •

The above perspectives bring a personal flavor to the deanship and likely reflect the thinking of many more deans than those quoted. One thing learned from the interviews is that many of the rewards associated with the dean's position are the ones one would expect to come from helping people achieve their potential. Another discovery is that the rewards experienced by deans are similar to those experienced by presidents. A number of presidents referred to the thrill they get from the graduation ceremony; some enjoyed talking with faculty and students; others in working with the community. Presidents, unlike deans (not surprisingly), pointed to the satisfaction they receive from reaching the top of their profession (Vaughan, 1986, p. 100–102). Presidents (p. 102) rarely referred to the rewards one would think would be inherent in being a part of something bigger than one's self, of playing a key role in achieving the nation's dream of universal higher education. On the other hand, several of the deans tended to feel that their role was important because of the contributions it made to the larger picture, especially in relationship to helping students. (Ironically, deans tend to think in terms of embodying the larger picture more than presidents, who tend to focus on personal accomplishments and failures.) In any event, deans, as is true with presidents, find their position satisfying, and those deans who assume the presidency should continue to reap many of the rewards they enjoy as deans.

### Frustrations

While rewards are inherent in the dean of instruction's position, so are frustrations. As with most administrative positions, deans find that their time is taken up with having to perform relatively trivial tasks. One dean sums up this frustration in a way that most community college administrators, including presidents, understand.

*It seems that a great deal of a dean's role is handling complaints. Sometimes they're easy to handle, sometimes they're not. For the people coming into the office with a complaint, it's a top priority, but it may be a very insignificant piece of your day. However, you have to treat it as something very important, and sometimes that is difficult to do. That gets a little frustrating.*

• • •

Time, or the lack of it, is the bane of deans of instruction, as it is for most administrators. One dean who has an open-door policy finds that "I tend to let almost everyone come into my office." Another dean describes his position as "the kind of position in which there are so many things to do that sometimes you're frustrated because you can't do them all." The same dean notes that "there is so much work to do in the position that your work is never really done. I think you need to take a long-range view. Sometimes you want to get things done, or at least I do, within a short period of time, and you have to realize that oftentimes things that are important are going to take a lot longer. You're going to have to involve a lot of people." The dean quoted above who wanted to know if she were going to be asked what she did not like about the position gave this answer: "The things I don't like? I hate the clerical part of administration, and there's so much of it. I just hate that. The major frustration is that you get something knit up on Monday, and by Wednesday it's unraveled and you have to knit it up again. My major frustration is in thinking you have something headed in one direction, and then it all comes apart and you've got to go back and put it together again. That is the major frustration."

As with time, the lack of resources was a source of frustration for a number of deans. One dean shared his frustrations on the lack of money:

*There is one great envy I still have of the four-year colleges. If we had, here at our college or at any good community college, a couple of hundred million dollar endowments, there isn't anything that the University of _____ is doing that we couldn't do. I really mean that. I don't mean it in the sense of research; rather, I mean it in the sense of truly making a difference in our state. In our four-county region, most of the Black students who get any education at all get it from us. And that's a deeply ingrained problem in our society. But would Exxon give us $200 million like they gave Tulane? No. Would Coca-Cola give us $100 million like they gave Emory? No. You know if* *they did, we'd pay that back. And that's really a frustration; I wish I could get the money together.*

• • •

Another dean experienced one of her greatest frustrations when funds were cut. She explains:

*We asked everyone to look at ways in which computers can support instruction. They did such a good job that everybody came in with a full schedule, and I only had one computer lab. I have to find more computers. But, I just called my office today and found out that our county wants us to cut the budget by $300,000. So, people did what I asked—they found ways to support instruction with new technology— and now I can't deliver what they need. We'll find a way, but some of those people are not going to be able to use the resources as much as they'd like. So, that keeps me up in the middle of the night. How am I going to do that? I need to reward them for doing a good thing, and instead, I'm kind of taking something away.*

• • •

Another frustration results from having to depend upon other people. As one dean notes: "You need to depend upon people to do the work. You can't do it all by yourself. And so, you need to organize some folks to do it and oftentimes they let you down. They have their priorities. You feel you want to move at a certain pace and they're not coming along at the same pace with you—that would be another frustration I find with the position." In the same vein, another dean notes: "Well, naturally, the frustrations are that ultimately you don't make all of the decisions; you've got to work with the system. And, no matter where you are in the system,...you have to deal with the community, with the legislature, the board of trustees—all of those things—and usually you would like to move faster."

One dean finds that it is not only lonely at the top but lonely near the top also. She is frustrated over her lack of contact with people.

*I spend so much time shut away in the office dealing with numbers, dealing with program proposals which I know are essential, etc., but when I'm working on them, I don't feel like they have anything to do with education. The bureaucracy that we have to deal with—state education departments and so forth—they want everything a certain* *way. I don't necessarily think these things have anything to do with quality, but I have to put everything in the right language to convince other people, and that's **very** frustrating.*

• • •

As is true with rewards and satisfactions, many of the frustrations experienced by the deans are similar to those experienced by presidents, including dealing with internal politics. One dean is frustrated by "the whole process of campus politics." He observes that "we're political animals. Every campus has its political environment, its political configuration, and people use those kinds of behaviors to pursue their own special interests, and they don't contribute much to the common good." Further, just as is true with deans, presidents point to a lack of time and resources as a source of frustration. Not surprisingly, presidents found external pressures more frustrating than did deans. One president sums up outside pressures well: "The most frustrating thing is the politicalization of the community college. Not only the board, but the state and others feel they have an oversight responsibility. Keeping it all in balance is very frustrating" (Vaughan, 1989b, p. 64). Understandably, presidents feel more pressures from state legislators, local politicians, special interest groups, and the state's executive branch than do deans (Vaughan, 1986, pp. 66–78). Presidents, on the other hand, do not experience as many frustrations emanating from daily contact with faculty and students as do deans.

As in the case of the rewards associated with the dean's position, frustrations tend to follow common themes: a lack of time, limited resources, and dealing with internal pressures emanating from faculty. Also, as in the case of rewards, frustrations tended to grow out of the daily tasks associated with bringing a large number of intelligent, creative people together in a common cause while at the same time administering a complex office. The dean occupies a position that can influence the direction of the institution, a direction that often results in change. Bringing about change, especially in an academic institution, certainly has its frustrations as well as its rewards.

*Lines of Demarcation.* The type and degree of frustrations experienced by the deans and presidents provide a line of demarcation between the positions, although not a clear one: for example, frustrations experienced by presidents such as internal (special interest groups) and external (politicians) pressures clearly establish the president's office as the place on campus where the buck stops, for often the dean is not able to contain the pressures or be in a position to recognize fully the implications they have for the institution. Most frustrations experienced by deans relate more to the day-to-day operation of the institution, frustrations that the effective president gladly cedes to the dean. On the other hand, by suggesting that presidents experience more external pressures than deans does not indicate an absence of such pressures in the dean's position. One dean understands the difference well. His analysis:

> I think the major frustration, or one of them, has got to be trying to balance the different political forces. They are at work constantly— internally and externally. I think most deans, at least the ones I'm familiar with, probably are not as heavily involved as their presidents in external political forces, but they are certainly aware of them.

● ● ●

Being aware of pressures and having to deal with them are worlds apart. The dean cannot and should not deal with external pressures to the degree that the president does.

Perhaps one of the clearest lines of demarcation between the positions is the known versus the unknown. Those deans interviewed, while noting voids in their preparation, believed that they were well-prepared to be deans and, in many respects, saw the dean's position as involving many of the same things that they had been doing but in a larger and more complex arena. Presidents, on the other hand, almost always experience shock upon assuming the position, for the presidency, unlike the deanship, is a new position to them and rarely is viewed as an extension of the dean's position, of the division chair's position, or of any other position on campus.

In the case of both deans and presidents, however, the frustrations never seem to outweigh the rewards associated with the positions. Deans of instruction, and especially those whose goal it is to become a president, should, as suggested by the dean quoted above, be aware of external and internal political forces, for it is those forces that have the potential of forcing the college's mission in directions that are not endorsed by the governing board or the college's leadership team.

## SUMMARY

Interviews often result in generalizations by the individual being interviewed and by the person reporting on the interviews. Certainly the above discussion is selective in the information gathered and in the reporting of that information.

Generalizations and selectivity, however, do not lessen the value of the lessons that can be learned or diminish the need to gather qualitative information on the deanship. Through deans sharing their views on the preparation needed for the deanship, pointing to voids in that preparation, and discussing the rewards and frustrations associated with the position, one is able to understand the dean of instruction's position more fully. An examination of the survey data reveals the following:

• The professional pathway to the deanship leads most often from a teaching position, to a division chair or assistant deanship, and then to the chief academic officer's position. Forty percent of the current deans followed this traditional, academic route; others reported that immediately prior to becoming dean of instruction they had been deans of student services (9 percent), faculty members (12 percent), administrators or faculty members at four-year colleges (6 percent), deans or directors of community services (9 percent), department chairs (2 percent), and assistants to the president (2 percent). Four percent had made lateral moves, and the remainder came from any number of positions.

• Upon assuming their positions, deans of instruction rarely experience the shock that new presidents often feel when taking on the chief executive officer's role. Most deans report that their educational and professional backgrounds have adequately prepared them for their new responsibilities. When adjustment problems are reported, they usually focus on inadequate management training (usually lacking in the dean's academic backgrounds) and on the need to view the college from a broader perspective than was heretofore necessary.

• Not surprisingly, deans derive their greatest satisfaction from helping students achieve their goals, while frustrations stem from bureaucratic chores (often delegated from the president's office) and from the political difficulties inherent in trying to accomplish goals through a large organization of creative, independent-minded individuals, while at the same time administering a complex office. Most deans usually find satisfaction in their work, however, noting that they achieve a sense of accomplishment by making a contribution to an organization that changes people's lives for the better.

Current deans, presidents, board members, and all members of the college community should recognize that the dean's position is critical to the success of the institution and work to understand the position as fully as possible. Current deans should engage in introspection, constantly evaluating the dean's position in relationship to themselves and to the institution and share the results with members of the college community and other members of the profession. The above, while making no claim to universal truths, should provide a good starting point for evaluating the dean of instruction's position and understanding those who currently occupy the position. Moreover, by discussing the dean's position candidly, those deans interviewed show a knowledge of the position that should be shared in greater depth than has been done by any dean in the past. More subjective study needs to be done on the position by someone who occupies the position. One problem deans may experience in regard to studying the deanship in depth is that many of them are looking beyond the deanship to the presidency and perhaps would view studying a position they consider a temporary way station in their career as a waste of time and energy. Assuming this is the case, then it lies with those individuals who see the deanship as a fitting climax to their career to build upon my work in this book and continue to interpret the position for current and future deans. To do so will serve the community college and the nation well, for this volume is only a beginning in the process.

# PART II

■

*Female and
Minority Deans*

I f the community college is to achieve its potential in service to the nation in the 1990s and beyond, its leaders must increasingly come from women and ethnic and racial minority groups. The outlook for increasing the number of women in leadership positions is somewhat encouraging, for 21 percent of the 619 deans responding to the CLS are women. Chapter 5 discusses female deans, with much of the discussion based upon the information obtained from the Women's Survey (WS) [See Appendix 2]. The women deans responding to the WS indicated that they perceive few problems in performing their duties due to their gender, although the exceptions are worth noting.

The outlook for racial and ethnic minority leadership is not as encouraging as it is for women. Only 7 percent of the deans responding to the CLS are racial or ethnic minorities. Of these, 3.2 percent are Black; 1.8 percent are Hispanic; and 2.0 percent are members of other racial or ethnic minority groups.

In order to understand some of the issues and opportunities facing racial and ethnic minority deans of instruction, Black and Hispanic deans were surveyed. The Black deans were asked to respond to the survey identified in the following discussion as the Black Survey (BS) [See Appendix 2]; the Hispanic deans were asked to respond to the survey identified in the following discussion as the Hispanic Survey (HS) [See Appendix 2].

One source suggests that the rights of minorities were debated as an ethical issue in the 1960s and 1970s, but "in the forthcoming decade, the educational and social advancement of minorities must be viewed as a national vested interest issue that cuts at the core and basic welfare of the U. S. economy" (Thomas and Hirsch, 1989, p. 62). The need for additional racial and ethnic minorities in leadership positions has not gone unnoticed by community college leaders. The AACJC, with urging from two of its affiliate councils, the National Council on Black American Affairs and the National Community College Hispanic Council, recently recognized the need for placing more emphasis upon minority leadership. Meeting in Minneapolis August 3–5, 1989, the AACJC Board of Directors acknowledged the need for the community college to place additional emphasis upon increasing its already considerable commitment to serving minorities (Reinhard, 1989). The Board's discussion resulted in making minority concerns a plank in the AACJC's 1990 Public Policy Agenda.

While the emphasis placed upon minorities by the AACJC Board is important, another item of discussion from the Minneapolis meeting has the potential of bringing about significant changes in the leadership of the community college of the future. At the meeting, the Board agreed to establish a new leadership institute aimed at mid-level and senior administrators other than presidents. According to Dale Parnell, president of the AACJC, one of the purposes of the institute will be to "bring a new group of leaders into the work of the AACJC, and help prepare a new cadre of leaders for the future of higher education" (*The Community, Technical, and Junior College Times*, August 29, 1989, p. 4). If the AACJC is successful in serving minorities, the new leadership institute must make serving ethnic and racial minorities a top priority, with special emphasis on deans of instruction, for the surest and quickest way to enhance minority leadership is to prepare minority academic deans to move into the presidency as quickly, as efficiently, and as effectively as possible. Indeed, the dean of instruction's position, with its incumbent often headed for the president's office, should be the focal point of the new institute, for these deans should be role models for faculty, students, deans of student services and finance, and others who have as their goal the community college presidency.

## APPROACHES TO THIS STUDY

Two points should be made as a preface to the discussion of women and minority deans: (1) most community colleges are truly equal opportunity employers and do not discriminate on the basis of race, age, sex or other factors that are beyond the candidate's control; and (2) it is very difficult to obtain information on community college professionals, including deans of instruction, who are women or members of racial and ethnic minority groups. In regard to the latter, the AACJC's annual survey of community college administrators, for example, does not gather information that identifies the sex, race, or ethnicity of the respondents. Some assistance was received from the American Association of Women in Community and Junior Colleges, the National Council of Instructional Administrators, the National Council on Black American Affairs (NCBAA), and the National Community College Hispanic Council (NCCHC) in identifying their membership, assistance for which I am grateful. These councils are all affiliate councils of the AACJC.

The NCBAA and NCCHC provided a list of names used in surveying minority deans. In the case of Blacks, the 15 deans identified by the council (nine responded to the survey) is short of the approximately 20 Black deans responding to the dean's CLS. (Assuming the number of deans (619) responding to the CLS is an accurate sample of the 1,169 identified for the survey, then approximately 38 of the current chief academic officers in the nation's community colleges are Black, making the 15 deans surveyed even less representative of all Black deans of instruction.) In the case of Hispanics, the 15 deans surveyed (14 responded) exceed the approximately 11 Hispanic deans responding to the deans' CLS and approaches 21 Hispanic deans (making the same assumption as is made regarding Blacks) out of the 1,169 deans surveyed. In addition, other than Blacks and Hispanics, no other ethnic and minority deans have such affiliate councils; the discussion on minority deans therefore is limited to Blacks and Hispanics, although 2 percent of the deans responding to the CLS survey are from other ethnic and racial minority groups.

The following three chapters are based, in part, upon the information obtained from the WS, the BS, and the HS. In the case of Blacks and Hispanics, the information is limited somewhat by the number of surveys analyzed. Indeed, due to the small number of deans responding to the BS and HS, no attempt is made to analyze the data in relationship to such things as family background, educational attainment of the deans, age, and other facts that are discussed in the chapter on female deans. Nevertheless, in spite of its limitations, a discussion of minority deans greatly enhances our understanding of the dean's position, especially in relationship to Hispanics and Blacks, two groups that must increasingly assume more positions of leadership if the community college is to fulfill its promise of serving all segments of society.

A discussion of women, Blacks, and Hispanics is important for reasons that go beyond the dean's position, for the deans and future presidents in these groups will serve as role models and mentors for future community college leaders as well as for future leaders in all segments of society. The need to serve as role models and mentors has long been viewed as an important part of the leadership role of these groups. A Black female dean states the case well for both minorities and women: "We DO have a responsibility to be the best we can be because we DO represent millions of others who have not gotten the opportunity to sit where we do" (Wheelan, n.d., p. 6; Wheelan is quoted in more detail in Chapter 5). While filling the roles of mentor and role model is nothing new to many women and minority deans, it is nevertheless helpful to determine how these deans view this aspect of leadership, for women and minority community college leaders can expect increasing pressure on them to devote more time and energy to this aspect of their role as the number of minority students (female students attending community colleges already outnumber male students) entering higher education, and especially those entering the community college, increases.

In addition to the surveys, Chapters 4, 5, and 6 draw upon *Leadership in Transition* (Vaughan, 1986) for comparisons of women and minority deans with women and minority presidents. Indeed, essentially the same type of information was gathered on both deans and presidents in order to provide the basis for such a comparison. For example, under the section entitled "The Asexual Deanship" in Chapter 4 and the sections entitled "The Aracial Deanship" in Chapters 5 and 6, the questions on which the sections are based are identical except that race and ethnicity are substituted for gender. The following explanation of this particular question avoids the necessity of repeating it in the three chapters. The basis of the question: Clark Kerr and Marian Gade (1986) concluded in *The Many Lives of Academic Presidents* that while women experience special problems in getting appointed to the presidency, once appointed, "Overall, they say they are more readily accepted as time goes on and, 'net' are not in any better or worse situation than men once they have been appointed..." (p. 118). The question: In essence, once someone assumes the presidency [according to Kerr and Gade], the assessment of performance becomes asexual (aracial). Do you agree with Kerr in relationship to the dean's position? If not, please explain how the assessment of the position is different for you because you are a woman (Black, Hispanic).

Section II of this volume is devoted to an examination of those deans who are women, Blacks, and Hispanics because to understand the community college of the future, leaders must begin to understand the roles members of these groups play now and must play in the future. It is hoped that this brief look will aid in the process of understanding these important leaders.

# 4

# Female Deans

## George B. Vaughan and Mary Lou Klaric

■

ecently, while attending the Association of Community College Trustees' annual meeting in Vancouver, B.C., the first author of this chapter was approached by a woman from a Southeastern state who was aware of some of the work that he had done on the community college presidency. With a somewhat bemused look on her face, she proceeded to share with him the details of an incident that had occurred to her less than one hour before their chance meeting. Her story: Crossing the lobby of the convention center, she noticed a group of five or six men talking and laughing, certainly not an atypical activity for people who attend conventions. Recognizing one of the men, she decided to go over to say hello. As she approached the group, she picked up the gist of the conversation. It seems that the convention planners had made some mistakes on the identification badges included in the convention packets. For example, one member of the group, the chair of the board of one of the colleges represented at the meeting, was laughing as he led the conversation: "Well," he exclaimed, as he pointed to his name tag, "I'm now a college president." As the woman approached the group, the board chair interrupted his conversation to greet her, although she was a stranger to him. In order to put a name with the face of the new arrival, he glanced quickly at her name tag. In a voice that showed obvious satisfaction in being able to build upon his interrupted conversation, he exclaimed gleefully: "Looky there, they've made her tag up wrong, too. It says president on it." Of course, anyone who has read this far knows the punchline: the woman was (and is) a president.

Did the female president exaggerate? We think not. She gave this chapter's first author permission to repeat the story, including the use of her name and college, and even gave him her office phone number. In order to protect the innocent (naive would be a better word to describe the trustee), we decided to keep her identity a secret. Indeed, identifying the president would detract from her symbolic role for female community college professionals who still suffer an identity crisis.

Establishing one's identity if one is a woman is not limited to community college presidents. For example, the *Washington Post* reported on the results of a survey of the most highly paid ($65,994 to $77,500) women employed by the federal government. Sixty-five percent of the women responding to the survey did not believe that their views were taken as seriously as those of men; 63 percent said that they had been mistaken for secretaries at meetings and had even been asked to fill the coffee pot and to take notes; 50 percent felt that men resented receiving orders from them; 33 percent believed that their personal lives were subject to more severe scrutiny than were the lives of their male counterparts; and 26 percent stated that being a woman hurt, rather than helped, in moving up the administrative ladder (cited in Vaughan, 1989a, p. 20).

*Time*'s December 4, 1989, cover story is entitled, "Women Face the '90s." It observes: "In the '80s they tried to have it all. Now they've just plain had it." It then asks: "Is there a future for feminism?" The inside story captures many of the frustrations and triumphs of women in the 1980s. One quote seems appropriate to set the stage for a discussion of female deans of instruction: "In many ways, feminism is a victim of its own resounding achievements. Its triumphs—in getting women into the workplace, in elevating their status in society and in shattering the 'feminine mystique' that defined female success only in terms of being a wife and a mother—have rendered it obsolete, at least in its original form and rhetoric" (p. 82). Certainly, the female deans have gotten into the workplace and have elevated their status in relationship to other community college professionals. They also provide rich territory for examining the deanship through the eyes of the majority of those women who currently occupy this important position.

A number of questions relating to women in the deanship can be asked, which, if answered, should help one to understand the position more fully. Among the questions asked on the survey were the following: Is there a woman's perspective on the dean of instruction's position?

Are there some assets associated with being a female dean? What has been the impact of affirmative action for women who hope to secure a deanship? Is the deanship asexual? These and other questions are explored as the position is viewed through the eyes of 129 female deans of instruction.

## BACKGROUND

Approximately 21 percent of the 619 deans responding to the CLS survey were women. While the AACJC does not collect information on the sex of chief academic officers, it does collect the addresses of its member institutions and, if possible, the names of the approximately 1,169 individuals occupying the position. The names were examined and a list was created of chief academic officers with first names normally associated with women. No attempt was made to determine the sex of those on the list who used initials or who had names that are commonly used by both sexes, nor was any attempt made to attach names to those labels that listed addresses only. The list yielded 187 names; surveys were therefore sent to those 187 individuals. Ten of the surveys were returned because the individuals no longer occupied the position (they moved to another institution, now are chief executive officers, or were in the position on an interim basis) and one was returned because, despite the efforts to include only females, the dean to whom it was sent is male, leaving 176 female deans in the pool. Of the 176 female deans who were sent the survey, 129 returned it, for an overall response rate of 73 percent. It should be pointed out that the response rate for all but two of the questions on the Women's Survey (WS) was at least 93 percent, although most had response rates ranging from 96 to 100 percent. The two questions that had the lowest response rates were the following: (1) What were your most important non-professional contacts external to the campus that helped you become a dean? and (2) What were the most important professional associations and organizations that aided you to become a dean? The response rates for those two questions were 82.9 and 89.1 percent, respectively. It is possible that no response for these two questions meant that no non-professional contacts and professional associations aided those deans in securing a deanship, for, as will be mentioned in more detail later in this chapter, the response from a large number of the deans to both of these questions was "none." Despite the response rate for those two questions, we believe that the results fairly represent the female deans in the pool as a whole and, as such, decided that it would not be necessary to provide the specific response rate for each question when the findings are presented. Instead, the findings are presented in terms of percentages, which usually have been rounded to the nearest whole number, and, occasionally, the actual number of deans who responded to a question in a particular way is provided.

It also should be pointed out that it is highly unlikely that all of the female deans responding to the earlier CLS survey of deans responded to the WS, nor is it likely that all of the women responding to the WS responded to the earlier CLS. One result is that the statistics may vary slightly between the surveys.

Female deans are distributed throughout our nation's community colleges. The average size of the institutions at which they are deans is 3,620, whereas the average size of the institutions for the 619 deans responding to the CLS survey is 3,051, dispelling any beliefs that women are deans only in the smaller institutions. The range of institutions was staggering, with one dean listing only 8 students at her institution and another one listing 16,200.

## Family Background

In *The Community College Presidency* (Vaughan, 1986), I painted a picture of a group of individuals who had far outstripped the socio-economic background of their families to ascend to the top of their profession. The two indicators used in the study of the presidency were educational level of parents and parents' occupations. I referred to the community college presidency as the "blue-collar presidency." The same two indicators were used to help determine the family background of female deans of instruction.

The fathers of the female deans completed more years of formal education than did the fathers of the deans as a whole or the fathers of current community college presidents. Sixty-four percent of the fathers of the female deans of instruction have a high school diploma or less, although over 40 percent of their fathers did complete high school; over 2 percent have an associate degree; almost 18 percent have a bachelor's degree; 7 percent have a master's degree; and over 6 percent have a doctorate (includes those with a J.D. and an M.D.). The 64 percent compares with 77 percent for the fathers of the deans responding to the CLS, a percentage that includes the responses of a number of female deans. In contrast to the female deans and the deans as a whole, over 80 percent of the presidents' fathers have a high school diploma or less (Vaughan, 1986, p. 10).

The mothers of female deans also have more formal schooling than do the mothers of the deans as a whole and the mothers of current presidents; they also have more formal education than do the fathers of female deans. Fifty-five percent of the mothers of female deans have a high school diploma or less (39 percent of them completed high school); 11 percent have an associate degree; almost 19 percent have a bachelor's degree; over 6 percent a master's; 1.6 percent a doctorate; and 7.7 percent hold other degrees, including nursing degrees and diplomas and business school diplomas. The 55 percent for the mothers of female deans (those with a high school diploma or less) compares to approximately 78 percent for the mothers of current presidents (Vaughan, 1986, p. 10) and approximately 73 percent for the mothers of the deans as a whole.

Even though the educational level of the mothers and fathers of female deans is higher than that of the parents of the deans as a whole and of presidents, the educational background of the parents of the female deans differs from that of the parents of the deans as a whole and of the presidents in degree and not in kind. The blue-collar deanship, while a paler blue, remains intact when examined through the educational level of the parents of female deans of instruction.

**Parents' Occupations**

Approximately 69 percent of the fathers of community college presidents engaged in occupations normally classified as blue collar. Sixty percent of the presidents listed their mothers' occupation as homemaker, with less than 10 percent listing occupations for their mothers that require at least a bachelor's degree (Vaughan, 1986, p. 11). Approximately 25 percent of the deans responding to the CLS listed a managerial or professional occupation for their fathers. The remaining 75 percent fell into the blue-collar classification. As for the occupation of their mothers, 48 percent of the CLS respondents listed homemaker, and over 10 percent listed professional positions (predominantly in education) that require a bachelor's degree or above (Vaughan, 1989b, p. 113).

Of the female deans responding to the WS, approximately 29 percent listed occupations for their fathers that fall within the managerial-professional class, those which normally require a bachelor's degree or higher (one listed her father's occupation as community college president!). The remaining 71 percent fell into the blue-collar classification. Homemaker still was the most common occupation for the mothers; however, the percentage of the mothers of female deans whose most recent occupation was that of homemaker (34 percent) was considerably lower than it was for the mothers of the deans as a whole and for the mothers of the presidents. Twenty-two percent of the mothers of female deans held positions in the education profession, 17 percent held clerical/secretarial positions, and 7 percent held positions in the nursing profession. The rest held various other types of occupations including owning or co-owning a business and positions in retail and real estate.

As with parent's educational level and despite the different distribution of occupations for the mothers of female deans, the occupations of the parents of female deans support the concept of the blue-collar deanship.

## Age and Tenure in Office

The average age of the female deans who responded to the WS is 49, with a range from 31 to 70; the average age of the 619 deans who responded to the CLS is 48.3. Does the average age of female deans indicate that they have moved along their career paths with the same speed as their male counterparts? Tenure in their current positions offers some clues: female deans on the average have been in their current positions for 3.6 years (60 percent have been in their current positions for fewer than 4 years); all deans, based on the responses to the CLS, have been in their positions for 5.4 years. Since a number of the female deans also responded to the CLS, thereby reducing the average number of years in their current positions for all deans, it is clear that female deans have been in their current positions for a fewer number of years than have all deans. Assuming the female deans have not changed positions any more often than the deans as a whole, one can conclude that, on the average, female deans assumed the deanship at a later age than did their male counterparts.

## Marital Status

Over 65 percent of the female deans are married, which compares with 87 percent for the deans who responded to the CLS; 12 percent of the female deans are single; 19 percent divorced; and 3 percent widowed. None of the female deans responding to the WS reported that they are separated from their spouses. While the 65 percent for female deans who stated that they are married is lower than the 87 percent for all deans (the 87 percent probably would have been higher if the female deans answering the survey were removed), there should be little doubt that many women are combining marriage with a highly demanding, and one would hope, rewarding career.

## Race

Almost 94 percent of the female deans responding to the WS are white; 3.1 percent are Black; 1.6 percent are Asian; and 1.6 percent are of Hispanic descent. Twenty-one percent of the deans who responded to the CLS are women, a figure that is considerably higher than the 7.6 percent of the current two-year college presidents (includes presidents of private junior colleges in addition to community college presidents) who are women (cited in Vaughan, 1989b, p. 115). Indeed, based upon the past, the future for women in terms of moving into the top community college leadership positions is brighter than it has been in the past. But the picture is less than bright for minority women for, as one can readily see, of the 129 women responding to the WS, only 4 are Black, 2 are Asian, and 2 are Hispanic.

## Mobility

Thirty-seven percent of the female deans answering the WS reported that they are deans in the state in which they had finished high school.[1] The 37 percent compares with 49 percent for all deans (those who responded to the CLS). However, deans as a whole and female deans in particular are more likely to move to another state than are community college presidents, for 45 percent of the presidents serve in the state in which they had finished high school (Vaughan, 1989b, p. 114).

## PREPARING FOR THE DEANSHIP

The dean of instruction's position is an important avenue to the presidency. Approximately 45 percent of the current presidents indicated that they were their college's chief academic officer prior to assuming the presidency (Vaughan, 1986, pp. 27–28). Forty-eight percent of the women responding to the presidential WS indicated that they were their college's chief academic officer prior to assuming the presidency (Vaughan, 1989b, p. 116). Obviously, if one is to use the academic deanship as an avenue to the presidency, one must first become an academic dean. What, then, are the pathways to the deanship?

For female deans, the pathway to the deanship is one with many branches, although the major pathways are the traditional ones of division chair, dean-director, vice-president, and assistant-associate dean. The division chair's position was the pathway most traveled by the female deans responding to the WS, with over 28 percent of the female deans stating that they occupied this position prior to assuming their first dean

---

[1] The percentage of female deans responding to the CLS who indicated that they lived in the state in which they had finished high school was almost 40 percent. The difference does not alter the situation: most female deans serve in states other than the one in which they had finished high school.

of instruction's position (29 percent of the deans responding to the CLS were division chairs prior to assuming their first deanship). Twenty-four percent of the deans had been deans or directors of various types, including dean of student services (8 previously held this position), dean of community services (2), and dean of finance (1), prior to assuming their first dean of instruction's position, and almost 20 percent were either assistant-associate deans or assistant-associate vice presidents (11 percent of the deans responding to the CLS were assistant or associate deans).

In addition to these pathways, 11 percent of the female deans came from any number of other campus positions; 7 percent were faculty members; and 4.7 percent came from positions outside the community college. Over 2 percent reported that they moved from one dean of instruction's position to another one.

## Academic Preparation

Seventy-three percent of the female deans responding to the WS have an earned doctorate, divided almost evenly between the Ph.D. (37 percent) and the Ed.D. (36 percent), and 25 percent have a master's degree. The remaining 2 percent (three deans) possess other degrees—an educational specialist degree, a J.D. degree, and a doctorate of arts in education. Thirty three of the deans (26 percent) have degrees in a discipline. Of those with a degree in a discipline, the largest number have degrees in English (8 deans or almost 25 percent of deans with a degree in a discipline); next are psychology, chemistry, and history, with 3 deans having their degrees in each of those disciplines. It should be noted that possession of an advanced degree does not mean that it was earned in a discipline, for 74 percent of the female deans responding to the WS have degrees in education, with over 43 percent having degrees in higher education.

The percentage for female deans with a doctorate (73 percent) is higher than the percentage for the deans who responded to the CLS (69 percent) but lower than the percentage for current presidents with a doctorate (76 percent). But these differences are not great enough for us to conclude that the academic preparation of deans is significantly higher for women than for men. Nor can we conclude that female deans have higher educational attainment than current college presidents.

## Professional Associations

The female deans were asked which, if any, professional associations aided them in becoming a dean. Over 31 percent of the deans who responded to this question answered "none," even though many of them belong to one or more such associations. Almost 69 percent listed one or more professional associations that they felt aided them in becoming a dean, and approximately 34 percent listed two or more professional associations. The organizations mentioned most often were the AACJC (listed by 23 deans), the American Association of Women in Community and Junior Colleges (16 listed it); the American Council on Education (ACE) (7 listed ACE and 6 listed ACE's National Identification Program); the American Association of University Women (7 listed it); and the American Association of Higher Education, which was listed by 6 deans. A number of state associations also were mentioned by the female deans as being important.

## Leadership Programs

The female deans were asked if they had participated in any leadership programs prior to becoming a dean that aided them in obtaining their positions. Sixty-three percent of the deans responding to this question on the WS said that they did not. Of the 37 percent who said that they did participate in a leadership program prior to becoming a dean, the most popular program was the Leaders for the '80s program, with 21 deans listing it; the next most popular was the ACE's National Identification Program, with 15 deans listing it; and 3 listed the Executive Leadership Institute sponsored by the University of Texas and the League for Innovation in the Community College. Harvard's Institute for Education Management, Bryn Mawr's HERS program, and ACE's Fellowship Program were each attended by two of the female deans. Numerous other leadership programs, some of which are limited to individual states, were mentioned by the deans. (The total number of programs in which the deans participated was higher than the number of those who answered "yes" to this question because several of the deans attended more than one leadership program.)

## External Contacts

The female deans also were asked to list their most important non-professional contacts that aided them in becoming a dean. Of those who answered this question, 41 percent stated that no external contacts played an important role in their becoming a dean. Fifty-nine percent listed at least one non-professional contact that aided them, and 26 percent listed two or more contacts external to the campus that were helpful. No single external organization stood out as being important, although 10 respondents listed the Chamber of Commerce. Many other organizations and individuals including community organizations; women's groups; national non-profit organizations such as the Girl Scouts, Red Cross and others; and family members and friends were mentioned. From this, it appears that many female deans are involved in their communities as good citizens as well as in their capacity as deans of instruction.

## Peer Networks

The WS asked if the deans were members of a peer group that aided them in becoming a dean. Sixty-seven percent of the deans answered that they did not belong to such a group. Of those who reported that they did belong to a peer group, 60 percent stated that the peer network was predominantly female, 31 percent belonged to predominantly male peer groups, and 9 percent belonged to peer groups comprised of both males and females with neither sex being predominant.

## Mentors and Role Models

Much has been written about the importance of mentors and role models, especially for women and minorities. How important were mentors and role models to women in their movement up the administrative ladder?

Mentors were important to current female community college presidents, with 75 percent pointing to a mentor as having influence upon their careers and 67 percent of those mentors being male (Vaughan, 1989b, p. 80). Seventy-one percent of the deans responding to the WS reported that they had a mentor who was important to their career. Of these, 76 percent indicated that their mentors were male, 11 percent had female mentors, and 13 percent stated that they had both male and female mentors.

Those mentors mentioned most often by the female deans were presidents (mentioned 33 times); deans (20); vice-presidents (16); and any number of other individuals ranging from professors, to "bosses," and colleagues.

How important are role models for future female deans? How often is one's role model and mentor the same person? When given a choice—which often is not the case in deciding one's mentor—did the female deans select a woman as a role model?

Fifty-nine percent of the female deans stated that they had a role model who influenced their career. Of these, 26 percent stated that their role model was also their mentor, 67 percent had a role model other than their mentor, and 7 percent had more than one role model, one of whom was their mentor.

Of those deans who had a role model other than their mentor, over 61 percent chose a female role model, whereas over 36 percent chose a male role model and 2 percent had both a male and female role model. The most popular role model was a college president (with 12 of the deans listing a president) followed closely by deans (11) and college professors (8). The remaining role models ran the gamut from mothers and fathers to professional peers.

Role models were important to a number of deans. For those deans whose role models were not their mentors, the majority chose a female role model, reinforcing the need for current female deans and presidents to be sensitive to the role they play in influencing others, especially women.

*Negative Role Models.* Given the choice, most community college professionals would likely choose a positive experience as a catalyst for changing their careers. On the other hand, negative experiences also can influence one's career. In an attempt to understand what negative experiences, if any, the female deans encountered, they were asked if they had a "negative role model" who influenced their career.

Fifty-five percent of the deans stated that they did not have a negative role model. On the other hand, 45 percent indicated that they had one, of which over 69 percent said their negative role models were males, over 20 percent indicated females, and over 10 percent had both male and female negative role models. Topping the list of negative role models were deans (24 of the deans mentioned a dean) and presidents (8).

Since negative role models often are supervisors and others in authority, and since males still tend to occupy those positions, the large number of male negative role models is not that surprising. The question remains: Were males negative role models because of their gender or because of their behaviors and performance on the job? And, would there be more female negative role models if more women were in leadership positions?

One female dean acknowledges the male dominance of the field in her response to the question of negative role models but, at the same time, offers some advice to all community college administrators. Her response:

> *Good question. Perhaps all ambitious women look at men in superior positions and know they could do the job as well—better. I saw tremendous ego problems in many male presidents. Women may not have fewer ego problems, but since I could only watch men at the top, I vowed to use the position of dean and president in the role of steward rather than king. Two specific presidents I have worked with convinced me that mental health and emotional health are as important as any other ingredient in these jobs and this career.*

• • •

The number of comments regarding negative role models are too numerous to repeat in their entirety here. By repeating some, however, the flavor of the comments is communicated. For example, one female dean's negative role model was a male dean of instruction who "was oppressive, overbearing, and who refused to allow differences of opinion." A female vice president did not consult with others who reported to her, set unreasonable deadlines, and was ineffective in serving as the chair of meetings. One female dean seemed especially prone to negative role models. "My whole professional life is and has been burdened by these negative role models. Middle-class white males with fragile, ego-strengthened world views have always populated the landscape of academe, so my agenda was to continue to do a better job. There have been a few good ones, however." Her negative ones often were "undemocratic," were "sexists" and "racists," and discriminated on the basis of a person's age.

Words and phrases that showed up often in the female dean's responses were "I knew I could do a better job," and the negative role model lacked communication skills and creativity, showed little concern for others, and was arbitrary, ego centered, and authoritarian. More than one female dean commented on "women who want to be like men," a characteristic that contributed to one of the dean's assigning a woman in this category to negative role model status. The negative role model, a professor, caused the dean to recall years later that "her negative qualities surely presented me with a picture of the type of woman leader I did *not* want to become. Her negative characteristics: her strong, forceful insistence on being one of the 'good old boys' in language (often vulgar) and demeanor (often aggressive); her habit of 'putting down' other people, especially women; her insensitivity toward others' feelings." Finally, one dean who worked under a female president discovered "a terrible ruthlessness and insecurity in the woman" who "did everything in her power to make my life miserable." As a result the dean reports that she "suffered a great deal, but I learned more from the suffering and more quickly than I probably could have otherwise. The experience changed me for the better in terms of how I administer and what I avoid."

By pointing out the negative aspects of leadership, it is hoped that others can learn what not to do. Moreover, by discussing negative role models, leaders are reminded that they do indeed live in glass houses and that often what is seen through its walls is not a pretty sight, especially when viewed by those who expect leaders to be positive models.

## OBTAINING THE DEANSHIP

Were female deans asked questions during interviews that were related to their gender? Do any of them feel that they ever lost a position because of their gender? What, if any, were the major obstacles encountered as a result of being a woman? Are there advantages that result from being a female dean? These were among the questions asked on the WS.

### The Interview

The number of deans who found being a woman either an asset or a liability during the interview process was almost equally divided, with 30 percent responding that gender was an asset and 29 percent stating that it was a liability; however, 27 percent felt that gender was not a factor. The remaining 14 percent either saw it as both an advantage and disadvantage or were not sure which it was.

*Assets.* Some of the responses regarding gender as an asset follow:

*When given a chance to ask a question of the president for the current position that I hold, I used the opportunity to my advantage. I asked the following question: 'Being a graduate of one of the leading community college leadership programs, I have spent considerable amounts of time studying the dynamics of leadership. One conclusion is that there are no real gender differences in the way effective leaders lead, yet I notice you have no women in leadership roles at your institution. Would you like to comment on that?' It did lead to an interesting dialogue.*

• • •

Another stated that "I feel it was an asset. I could be outgoing, energetic, and aware of my appearance [when meeting] with the committee. In this case it worked; it didn't always."

A number of deans felt that history was in their favor, for many institutions had few or no female administrators. One dean noted that she "was the only woman candidate and the most relaxed and enthusiastic." From another: "An asset: There were no women in higher administration at the college and they were being pressured to hire females. I was qualified, interested, and ready for the challenge." Similarly, "I believe it may have been an asset because I am the first woman to hold this position. This is a group of faculty who likes to keep up with the times." And a qualified response: "For me I felt it was an asset; all other candidates interviewed were male and there were several supportive women on the search committee, although I think the search committee's direct knowledge of my work was the strongest factor in my favor."

A number of the respondents made the point that they consider being a woman an asset in all of their endeavors. One dean's response presents this point of view well.

> My answer may not help, but this is it. I feel that being a woman is an asset in everything I do. I have had to hone my abilities to a greater degree than is required of males simply to compete. Being a female in an interview process would seem to me to permit me greater sensitivity to the nuances of the process and, therefore, greater likelihood of being successful.

• • •

Liabilities. The 29 percent of the deans who felt that their gender was a liability during the interview process offered a number of explanations as to why they felt that way. One believes that being a woman is never an asset when applying for a leadership position. From another: "It is a liability. I was the first female hired in a deanship. It took an appointment rather than a search to get me there." One dean, while stating that her gender was a liability, offers a comment that indicates the complexity of answering the question.

> Difficult question. My style was an asset, a more 'feminine' approach, team leader, reflective leader, etc. My coalition-building skills were valuable, and these skills are often seen as more 'feminine' in nature. These same skills, however, were probably [seen as] liabilities to some on the committee, as they were not the typical 'male' qualities they were looking for.

• • •

Another dean believes that, "In general, I think women have a more difficult time establishing credibility. Search committees seem more willing to take a chance on men." One dean views it as a liability, but hedges somewhat on her answer.

> A liability, but not to the degree I had previously believed it to be. Of the five other candidates (all male), two struck out, one found another job, two refused the salary offer. I was called last (as far as I know) and accepted the lowest salary. It should also be noted that the decision to offer the position to me ended the longest search (from the

*interview of the finalists to the actual offer) the institution has ever engaged in.*

• • •

One dean who saw being a woman as both an asset and a liability places the debate in perspective. "This is a really ambivalent question! Yes, I was given a chance because of my gender and the perception of the characteristics that I would bring. And I may have surprised some by my individuality. That same surprise may have become a liability because all of the stereotypical expectations are not true." And another who beat out some tough competition, both female and male, provides an adequate conclusion for the debate on assets versus liabilities. She notes that after doing well in the interview and getting the position, she found that, "Then, I suppose like everyone else, I had a year to prove that I could indeed do the job."

Only 17 of the deans answered "yes" when asked on the WS if any gender-related questions were asked during interviews for their current position. While the number who responded "yes" is relatively small, the comments of those deans who were asked gender-related questions offer insights into the selection process and into how some few members of the college community view women.

A number of the questions that were asked concerned the dean's family life. For example, one dean was asked who would care for her children when they became ill. Her response: "My husband." Another was asked "about my husband's job." And another was asked if her children would keep her from taking out-of-town trips and working long hours. A female faculty member asked one dean how her husband would manage if she moved to a different city. And a president wanted to know, "What will you do with your husband?" Another administrator observed that the applicant and future dean was a single parent. He wanted to know how she could raise children alone. A female faculty leader, who missed the formal interview, later told the successful candidate that she would have opposed her appointment because "a single woman with children cannot be a dean in this community." A trustee observed, "Since you have children, I assume there was a Mr. H_____ once." One woman who moved from faculty member to dean faced a number of questions which she found offensive and inappropriate:

*In the process of interviewing for the position, for which I was the only female applicant, I was asked a number of sexist questions which I quietly reversed and asked the questioner. The most persistent was a faculty member whose wife also taught. He asked me how I could expect to serve as dean while trying to raise children, run a house, and be a farmer's wife. I responded to his question with a comment that both he and his wife managed to accomplish a number of things and then mentioned that his question was inappropriate. Several of the other faculty members present at the interview were relieved that I addressed the inappropriateness of the question.*

• • •

In addition to questions relating to the candidate's family, some questions were asked regarding a woman's ability to function in the role. One future female dean was asked by a male administrator: "Are you tough enough to stand toe to toe with other vice presidents?" Both administrators and trustees expressed some concern over their future female dean's ability to "boss" the administrative team, over her ability to deal with the budget (she taught micro and macro economics for eight years), over her public speaking ability (she was an elected town official), and over her ability to make "hard" decisions.

While the number of female deans who were asked gender-related questions was small (an encouraging sign for community colleges as they work to overcome stereotyping associated with sex and for women seeking leadership positions in community colleges), the questions asked make it clear that gender is not a totally dead issue. However, keep in mind that in every case cited the applicant got the position.

In a follow-up question on the WS (Were any gender-related questions asked during interviews for positions that you did not get?), the vast majority of the deans who responded to the question (84 percent) again said "no." But 20 of the deans were asked gender-related questions, which further illustrates that during interviews women still may be asked questions that are unrelated to the requirements of the position and should be prepared to respond as professionally as possible to some rather personal questions, inappropriate though they may seem to be.

Did the female deans who were turned down for deanships prior to obtaining their current positions believe that they did not get those positions because of their gender? First, it is important to note that 66 percent of the deans who responded to this question reported that they had never been turned down for a deanship for which they applied. Of those who said they had been turned down for a deanship in the past, 35 percent felt that being a female candidate was responsible, at least in part, for their not being offered the position. Why did they feel that being a female was one of the causes for not being offered the position? Their answers are revealing.

From one dean: "Most people have been conditioned that males are appropriate in positions of leadership. It's hard for them to see a young, attractive female in the role. I feel I had to be twice as qualified as a male to get the same position." From another: "A committee member and the college president commented on my 'calm soothing voice,' a remark that they probably wouldn't have made to a male." Another candidate felt there was a perception among the faculty that her manner was "soft" and that she suffered from her failure to "show off" her literary knowledge. Another dean believes she lost the position because the college community felt that "we can't hire a female dean, we have a woman president."

Did those deans who lost positions really lose them because of sex stereotyping, or were they simply engaging in some healthy rationalizing? The answer is elusive. One dean speaks to the complexities of the question and the ironies often found in the selection process. "The job was given to a woman, but one who was a 'yes man.' I was deemed 'too independent.' This was stated publicly by the man who made the selection." She adds a postscript: "He was later demoted for propositioning a young female staff member who taped it."

As with race, questions regarding the sex of candidates are likely settled prior to the interview, for practical as well as legal reasons. The good news is that most of the deans were never turned down for a deanship and most were not asked gender related questions during interviews. But, as illustrated above, sex stereotyping may still exist and questions related to gender occasionally do creep into the interview process on some campuses. Women who aspire to the presidency as well as to deanships should be sensitive to these possibilities and be prepared to deal with sexual biases rationally, unemotionally, and professionally, remembering that both time and the courts are on their side.

## Affirmative Action

One of the legal answers to discrimination on the basis of race, ethnicity, and gender is affirmative action. The female deans were asked if affirmative action aided them in becoming a dean. Sixty percent said that it did not; 34 percent said that it did; the remainder provided "yes-no" and "maybe" answers. The answers of the deans (43 total) who felt that affirmative action helped them included the following types of responses: Affirmative action (1) forced employers to include women in the pool of candidates; (2) made it impossible to ignore women's qualifications; (3) brought about an awareness of women's assets; (4) demanded that women be treated seriously; and (5) made the process as fair as possible. The success of other women helped some of the female deans secure administrative positions. (Two comments illustrate this point: "I followed a successful female dean of instruction, and the president preferred another female in the position." "I followed a strong woman who...was popular with the faculty. The president who hired me likes to hire women [administrators] and recognizes our competence.") While the ages of all respondents were not analyzed in detail, it is interesting to note that, of the eight deans responding to the survey who are over the age of 60, none felt that affirmative action played a role in their obtaining the deanship.

A positive statement from one dean on the role of affirmative action suggests that the program has accomplished some of its objectives, at least as far as women are concerned. This dean noted that affirmative action aided her "for the first dean job in 1980 but not for the VP of instruction job in 1989. I would not have gotten a start in administration until much later; in fact, I would not have conceived of myself as an administrator and leader without affirmative action." On the other hand, one dean was told by the president that she got the job because she was a woman. Her reaction: "I thought I had been selected because I was a talented teacher."

Probably the major contribution of affirmative action is in assuring that women are included in the pool of applicants. Most women, once included in the pool, believe that they got the deanship because they were the right match for the position and because they were well qualified to be a dean. One dean made a comment about the employment of women that presidents should note, even when affirmative action programs exist. Her comment: "It is the courage and openness to change of the CEO or president that results in the hiring of women."

## Obstacles Encountered by Female Deans

Sixty-five percent of the female deans responded that they had encountered major obstacles on the pathway to the deanship as a result of being a woman. Some of the obstacles related to institutional culture, or at least to how the respondents viewed that culture. Among the obstacles that resulted from institutional culture were such things as not being taken seriously because of one's sex; men not wanting to work for women; lack of mentors and role models for women; having to face the "good old boys' network"; the perception that men, not women, belong in leadership positions; the initial inability to understand and use the "system"; the higher expectations demanded of women; coming from a "female" profession (nursing); lack of support from women in lower-level positions; the belief that it was a risk to hire a woman; and being viewed as a "women's libber" if one supports women's rights.

Biases resulting from institutional culture came in many packages. One dean encountered resistance from men who did not want "a woman boss." One male administrator counseled the president about the impropriety of traveling with a female dean. One dean found that because her teaching field was dominated by men and because department and division chairs were elected, she had difficulty in getting lower-level experience in order to qualify for an assistant dean's position. One dean stated: "The answer is very simple: the sexist practices of an old boy system." Another dean was haunted by the "perception that women cannot handle authority or the stress that comes with the position; by the perception that women let family responsibilities interfere with the job; and by the perception that women are too emotional." One dean found that an obstacle was that "as a woman with a male mentor you have to prove that you didn't sleep your way to new opportunities." She also found that she worked so hard to please everyone and do everything right, that she did not take the time to plan and market herself for a higher position. Another dean believes that "sometimes a woman is not viewed as seriously as a man. Input into the decision-making process is not given the same weight. Also, a female administrator is sometimes viewed as being unusual; therefore, men and women may have difficulty adjusting to a female supervisor." One dean noted that the major obstacle she faced was tradition, "I was the first female chief academic officer in [a particular state's] technical college system! Anything else paled in comparison to tradition."

Another group of obstacles resulted from cultural biases found in the larger society, especially those relating to the "place" of women within that society. Among the obstacles were having to put their career on hold to raise a family; being a single parent; having to deal with problems that can arise in a two-career family; growing up female and not being encouraged to have a career; and the unwillingness of spouses and other family members to relocate. The following observations by female deans serve to illustrate some of the difficulties they faced as a result of cultural biases.

One dean "needed to take out years to have children in an era when child care facilities were few and far between." One dean was unable to start her administrative career until age 42 because she had to raise her children first. Another one found that "disruptions and long commutes" held her back in her two-career family. One dean believes she was bypassed for promotions because she was married but not the family's principal breadwinner. Another dean notes that the length of time it took her to complete her Ph.D. because of family commitments hurt her career.

One dean faced a major obstacle in her career because she was a single parent with an adolescent child and two children in college. A major obstacle for one dean was "being born in 1938 and growing up when a woman's role was at home, especially in the 1950s." Three of the deans felt that being "placebound" made it hard to pursue a top-level administrative position. Another dean notes that family obligations made serving as a dean difficult and suggested that "any woman aspiring to be in administration needs a househusband or supportive other who can be the primary caregiver." One dean captures the essence of the obstacles associated with the culture of the larger society.

> *The expectation when I graduated from college in 1959 was that a woman would work until she married or until she had children and then could stay at home to take care of the children. Therefore, women did not plan for careers. It was not until 1969 that I thought seriously about having a job (when I separated from my husband) and really not until 10 years after that I began thinking of a career path in higher education rather than a position as a faculty member. I had not been socialized to plan for a career as a child or student and only began to think seriously about my career fairly recently.*

● ● ●

## ASSUMING THE POSITION: ADVANTAGES AND DISADVANTAGES

Are there certain aspects of the dean's position that are made easier because the occupant is a woman? Is the reverse true? Or are the current female deans uncertain? Forty-four percent of those responding to the survey felt that being a woman made at least some aspects of their deanship easier. Fifty-three percent did not. The remainder were ambivalent.

### Gender: Easing the Way

Some female deans realize that they "are different," especially when working with men. One dean commented on the broader aspects of being a woman and occupying the dean's position, stating her belief that "consciousness is raised" regarding equal opportunity for women and minorities. She adds a regional flavor to her relationship with her male colleagues:

> *I also think the Southern male tradition of 'treating a lady well,' which can be difficult to overcome, but which must be overcome, can make*

*the job easier [for a woman]. Men sometimes let their guard down*
*if they consider the woman to be of little consequence or 'fragile'; this*
*allows the woman to be effective without the resistance a male might*
*encounter.*

• • •

Similarly, minus the pedestal: "I sometimes think I get away with more
because men don't want to hurt my feelings." From another, "Faculty
seem less ready for battle [because of my gender]." Another dean notes
that "By and large, since most male colleagues and supervisors do not
perceive of themselves as having any gender bias, you can use that to
your professional advantage." And, from another dean: "Most of the men
try harder than they might with a male." Finally, "Men go out of their
way to explain some things to me such as architectural and mechanical
drawings. Most of these things are very simple to understand. However,
I have the advantage of not being expected to know. I don't find this
demeaning but humorous."

The female deans offer an interesting perspective on working with
other women, especially members of the support staff. Many of the comments go against much of the popular mythology that women do not
like working for and with other women and add to the understanding
of the female dean. "[My gender provides me with] the ease of working
with female staff; the ability to build relationships and expect (and get)
honest feedback; [it also provides me with] entree to the women's room."
In relationship to the staff, one dean notes that "I think the clerical and
the female custodial staff often find me less threatening [than men] and
will confide in me more easily." Likewise, from another dean: "Classified staff, mostly female, relate more easily to another woman." And from
another dean, "I have developed excellent rapport with other women,
especially clerical support staff. I hold the same values regarding family
priorities that they do, and this creates a bond. Women faculty also appreciate my support, as do women students." Last, "Many situations involving support staff were more easily resolved because the secretarial
staff believed I understood the problems because I am a woman."

The greatest number of comments came from deans about what they
perceive are female characteristics that enhance their effectiveness. The
following quotes are from different deans. "I can say 'I'm sorry' or 'I care'
more easily than I perceive a man can or does." "In general, I find it easy
to listen to others, to ask for and use advice and suggestions from others.
These and other aspects of interpersonal communications, I feel, are part
of the skills many women bring to their jobs. Also, most women are less

competitive and less interested in 'game playing' and 'turf battles' than their male counterparts." "People respond to warmth and open communications." "Generally speaking I believe women nurture more naturally and deal with personnel issues more interpersonally." "I find that I am less threatening in a power position because women are viewed as less egocentric." "Generally, I think women have better listening skills than men and are able to handle volatile situations more effectively." "[Women are better at] moderating discussions that become emotional and getting everyone 'calmed' down." "I sincerely believe I am more sensitive to the needs of faculty than were the males who were dean before me." "Equanimity and wisdom born of years of being a 'gal.' Those who grow up without power learn the power of collaboration very well, sports or no sports." "I think women roll with the punches a little easier than men do because the job isn't as closely attached to a female ego or self-image." "I think women are assumed to be more nurturing and thus would have the interests of people at heart." "[Women] can be more persuasive, more frank without being threatening." "I do believe that women may be uniquely prepared to help develop a healthy therapeutic environment on campus." "I sincerely believe women are more open in their communications, which keeps down rumors and misunderstandings." "[Women are better at] showing empathy and dealing personally and warmly with others—peers, faculty, and students."

Certainly the above quotes have much to say about the way many women view their roles as leaders. Perhaps inadvertently, the above comments also make important statements on how some male deans approach positions of leadership. Certainly male deans and presidents should take note as should governing board members of both sexes.

## Gender: Some Complications

As mentioned above, 62 percent of the female deans feel that the dean's position is more difficult because they are women. Their comments point to some of the difficulties. Some of the complications of being a female dean have been discussed above under the section on the liabilities associated with being a female spouse, mother, and in general suffering from the "Wonderwoman syndrome." For example, one dean notes that it is very difficult "balancing the career with demands of children and a husband, for there are not enough hours or energy to be as good as we want!" From another, "I do not have a spouse to provide 'social services.' I have to live away from my husband during the week because he couldn't leave his job." And from another: "[There is the] need to balance responsibilities to my family and young children, including car pooling, etc., which I enjoy but most male deans who are fathers don't need to do or want to do."

Male deans may well argue correctly that they too have family responsibilities that take their time and energy (mowing the lawn versus car pooling) away from their roles as deans. However true as the male argument is, it is well documented that an inordinate number of family responsibilities often fall upon the female spouse.

The ever-present male-female relationship complicated the deanship for some of the female deans. One dean notes that she has some problems with "men who flirt before getting down to business." Another has some difficulty "working one-on-one and socializing with male faculty." Another finds "dealing with sexist males and females who prefer male bosses" to be a problem. Another is bothered by the "inside jokes of the old boys' network."

The double-standard is perceived as a problem by some deans. One believes that "when I'm tough, I'm perceived as a bitch. When my boss (male) is tough, he's a good businessman." Another dean feels the same: "The adage applies: if a man is 'tough' he's decisive; if a women is, she's a 'bitch.' The toughest thing for a woman in command of a male staff is being in charge without being dictatorial, whiney, or flirting with one of the boys. It is very difficult to be 'boss' and not lose some sense of your feminine self." Similarly, another notes that "it has taken time to learn to be an SOB, not with my staff but with my peers." Another female dean "won't talk about football or other sports during staff meetings. There is little genuine colleagueship and support from others on my level." While not considering it a serious problem, one dean notes that "men aren't as comfortable about kidding around when I'm present. I do believe a woman must be especially careful in her relationships with male peers and supervisors so as not to give any perception of impropriety." One dean, who dislikes reprimanding anyone, finds that "it is particularly distasteful to reprimand a male. Conflict is not the issue. I am simply too conscious of the 'male ego' and what a reprimand from a woman may be doing to that male ego. That consciousness creates more discomfort for me than it should."

While, as one female dean suggests, many of the issues related to the female-male relationship "may be *my* problem as a woman," the fact remains that many women perceive their effectiveness to be impeded by their relationships with their male colleagues. It behooves every member of the campus community to be sensitive to the needs of the other sex and eliminate those aspects of relationships that cause members of either sex to perceive barriers resulting from that relationship.

Another area of concern for some women relates to community contacts. As one dean observes, "It is more difficult to establish connection in the community with businessmen, many of whom do not acknowledge the existence of women in significant roles. For example, I have stood with the president of the college and the business manager, both males, and have watched a businessman greet the male on my left, skip me entirely, and greet the male on the right." Another feels she has a problem because she cannot "gain access to all-male groups in the community." Another believes that "the difficulty is external to the college. I have noticed during economic development activities or in working with advisory committees that male representatives. . . are taken aback initially by the fact that I am a woman." Three deans mentioned those great bastions for "male bonding," the locker room and the Rotary Club. From one: "The inability to participate in major community organizations (Rotary, Lions, etc.) and the inability to [engage] in informal dialogue (locker room talk) with subordinates, who are all men" presents some problems. Another simply refers to the Rotary and "the locker room before and after games" as limiting her ability to perform her duties somewhat.

If female deans are barred, or are perceived to be barred, from important community activities, then indeed the community college will suffer in the future. Especially damaging will be the inability of female deans to gain valuable experience in working with community groups, experience that would be a major asset should they assume the community college presidency.

## THE ASEXUAL DEANSHIP

The final question regarding being female and occupying the deanship dealt with the asexual nature of the position. Is the dean's position, once one is in that position, asexual? Fifty-nine percent of the female deans believe that it is; 37 percent disagree; the remainder are unsure.

### The Deanship is Asexual

Although those responding in the affirmative to the question were not asked to comment, some did, and their comments are revealing. While one dean feels that she attracted attention initially because of her gender, she agrees with Kerr and Gade that "this dissipates with time." Another believes that it is up to the dean and the president to keep "femaleness" out of the picture. One dean subscribes to rule number one: "I feel performance is the ultimate test." Another dean notes that "expectations are high. Standards are tough ones. I'm expected to meet them regardless of my sex. It is irrelevant." One other respondent agrees with Kerr and Gade but with reservations. She notes that she thinks "others assess you by performance once you are in the role. However, I find I put extra 'requirements' on myself to demonstrate my effectiveness. It is as if you never get over the feeling of having to 'prove yourself,' just in case someone remembers you are female." Finally, one dean speaks to the evolutionary nature of the deanship and of society. Her observations regarding the asexual deanship:

> When women first were appointed deans and presidents, I believe they were evaluated on the fact they were female. I do not believe that is the case in 1989; there are at least 10 women deans or vice presidents in the academic area in the [state] community colleges, three women presidents, and numerous deans/vice presidents in other areas. I truly believe that they are (for the most part) evaluated on their performance. When women signal the fact that they are female and imply that they expect different treatment, then they may be evaluated on the basis of being a woman.

• • •

Finally, from another dean: "Once you reach the top, the view is different. You forget the struggle. You are accepted because you hold the power."

## The Deanship is Not Asexual

Thirty-seven percent of the female deans (47 respondents) believe that the deanship is not asexual, a concept that had negative connotations for most of the 47 women. The following comments reinforce much of what has been said earlier and make it clear that perceived sexual biases continue to trouble some women, even after they become a dean. The following comments are from different deans.

"Many female leaders, who are not themselves Queen Bees aping the male model, tend to favor collaborative, process-oriented decision-making, which often isn't highly regarded by traditional males." "I think how you perform is, of course, very critical in how you are evaluated—perhaps the most critical variable. However, I think females are always evaluated more critically than males." "I think women are more closely watched to see if they can perform." "There are always enough sexists (and outright misogynists) around whose patriarchal styles do not allow for fair evaluation of women's work. Sadly, there are enough 'Queen Bees' in the world to serve to ensure the stereotypic perceptions of women." "In the case of a woman there is not room for error in judgment or lack of performance. The standards seem to be different for men and women. Women are expected to work longer hours, and their assignments have to be flawless. This is not always the standard for men." "Women in this state are judged as 'retarded men' in the upper echelon. Women presidents or chancellors don't last long in the public arena here."

One dean places the issue of the deanship in a perspective that clearly shows that she believes the position is not asexual but that she does not see that as either negative or positive.

> I don't agree with Clark Kerr period. Some will always have difficulties working with a woman. Others will work better with me because I am a woman. I could rationalize all of my problems and blame it on my sex but I don't believe that to be true. I feel that while gender may affect how people relate to you, a successful administrator is viewed as successful by most of his or her critics regardless of gender. I know there are faculty who will never support what I do, and that may be because I am a woman. However, I also know that my male predecessor had difficulties, and many more of them than I have. It comes with the job. It is impossible to determine whether any or all of our problems were related to being female.

• • •

## ADVICE FROM FEMALE DEANS

The WS asked the respondents what advice they would offer other women interested in pursuing the deanship. Many of their responses are good advice for anyone interested in moving up in the administrative ranks, i.e., get the doctorate, have a sense of humor, be a team player. The primary purpose of asking the question, however, was to seek the advice current female deans would offer other women that might help them view their gender through a perspective that would aid them in obtaining a deanship. Some of the answers follow.

> Don't become discouraged if you detect that men are resistant to working with or for you. Hard work and good preparation generally overcome most obstacles.

• • •

*Avoid attributing all of your difficulties in working with men to the male-female 'situation.' Assume initially that men want to work in good faith with women and believe that two people—whatever their sexes—can work out problems if they deal with each honestly and openly.*

• • •

*Keep up your national networks.*

• • •

*Align yourself with peers who will support your efforts at seeking promotion—preferably females, but include non-sexist males.*

• • •

*Do not network exclusively with women.*

• • •

*Don't make being a woman an issue.*

• • •

*Don't be super-conscious of being a* woman; *be conscious of being a competent, intelligent, objective, humane person.*

• • •

*Do not be afraid to deal with your femininity and your ability—they are not mutually exclusive.*

• • •

*Know who you are as a person, apart from male or female. Be true to that person.*

• • •

*Use the existing support systems for women for continuous, positive feedback and assistance.*

• • •

*Anticipate and defuse situations that may arise relating to the sex of those involved.*

• • •

*Approach the position as a dean, not a woman dean or a male dean.*

• • •

*Don't constantly be on the lookout for discrimination, it puts people at a distance.*

• • •

*Don't be held back or spurred on by your gender. Ignore it and do the best damn job you can.*

• • •

*Never use your sex as an excuse; don't hide behind your own skirt!*

• • •

*Be prepared for major adjustments in your personal life. Your husband and children will require a lot of patience and independence.*

• • •

*Get some help in personal matters—a maid, child care, etc.*

• • •

*Be yourself. Don't try to fit into a male mold.*

• • •

*Don't assume male personality characteristics as a defense.*

• • •

*Keep your feminine traits of caring, communicating, and offering kind words whenever possible. Don't try to be a man, be a good dean of instruction.*

• • •

*Be aware that you are 'breaking ground.' You will probably be lonely, highly pressed, frequently tested, and overworked. Be patient with yourself and others. Having 'ordinary' women in leadership positions is new to everyone.*

• • •

*Don't give up. Competent women and minorities are needed. Hang in there; persistence and talent do come through (sometimes).*

• • •

# SUMMARY

When I surveyed the population of deans of instruction in 1987, approximately one-fifth (21 percent) of the respondents were women. In one sense, this result was discouraging, underscoring the fact that women, who constitute 53 percent of all community college students, remain a minority in the college's administrative ranks. But when one considers that women account for approximately 8 percent of community college presidents (Green, 1988, p. 4), the participation in the dean's survey appears quite encouraging indeed. For if the deanship is truly the primary route to the presidency, then the next generation of community college presidents—all things being equal—should include an unprecedented number of women.

But will the relatively large number of female deans actually find that the doors to the presidency are open? In order to investigate this and other related questions, I followed up the dean's survey with a special survey of female chief academic officers. The major findings, summarized below, suggest that gender figures heavily, and sometimes negatively, in their career advancement.

- In terms of socioeconomic background, demographic characteristics (including age), and position held prior to being named dean of instruction, female deans are quite similar to their male colleagues. Nonetheless, salient differences emerge in terms of their personal lives. Women are significantly less likely to be married than the population of deans as a whole (65 percent versus 85 percent, respectively) and more likely to be mobile (only 37 percent of the women held deanships in the states in which they obtained their high school diplomas, compared to 49 percent of the deans as a whole).

- In addition, it appears that women assume the deanship at a later age than men. Though the average age of male and female deans is approximately the same, the average length of tenure in their current positions is shorter for women (3.6 years for women, compared to 5.4 years for the population of deans as a whole).

- The age discrepancy between male and female deans may be a factor of the difficulties women appear to encounter on the pathway to the deanship. While three-quarters of the female deans had helpful mentors or role models (the majority of whom were male), most of the female deans (65 percent) said that they had encountered major obstacles on the path to the deanship as a result of their gender. About the same proportion of female deans (60 percent) indicated that affirmative action had not aided them directly in attaining their current positions.

• Female deans did not always feel that their gender was a professional liability. When asked if gender played a role during the interview for the deanship, the majority of female deans (59 percent) said yes; 30 percent indicated that their gender was an asset; another 29 percent said it was a liability. Whether viewed as a detriment or an asset, however, it is notable that most of the female deans did not view gender as an irrelevant factor in the interview process.

• While a majority of the female deans agreed with the assertion that the deanship is asexual, with women and men evaluated equally on the basis of performance, 62 percent nonetheless indicated that their gender made it more difficult for them to carry out their jobs.

Thus, while it appears that a growing number of women are advancing on the pathway to the presidency, that pathway still is rougher for women than it is for men. However, as the next two chapters will show, Black and Hispanic men also encounter special difficulties along their career paths.

# 5

# Black Deans

■

As suggested in the introduction to this section, information on Black deans is somewhat limited. On the other hand, information on Black presidents can help in understanding Black deans. For example, one problem Black presidential candidates encountered was in being perceived as suited to serve as the president of urban, predominantly Black institutions but not suited for predominantly white, suburban ones. As reported in *Leadership in Transition* (Vaughan, 1989b), one Black president noted that, "I was channeled into a stereotyped urban institution serving minorities. There is no real access to a range of institutions for Black presidents" (p. 88). Similarly, another president reported that, "Having reached the level of dean, the only institutions interested in employing me [as a president] were predominantly Black institutions" (Vaughan, 1989b, p. 88). Did deans of instruction encounter similar stereotyping on their pathway to the deanship?

## THE INTERVIEW

Only a small number of the Black presidents were asked questions relating to race during the interview. One conclusion reached by this author was that if race is to be an issue (either an advantage or disadvantage) in the presidential selection process, the issue has been settled prior to the interview. For example, if a Black is interviewed for an inner-city, predominantly Black institution, being Black may be an advantage, and therefore race is not an issue in the negative sense (Vaughan, 1989b, pp. 39–90). Were Black deans treated similarly?

The deans were asked on the Black Survey (BS) if being Black helped them in obtaining an interview for the deanship, and if any questions related to their race were asked, either during the process that resulted in their current position or in previous interviews for a deanship. Commenting on questions related to race in interviews, one dean replied that, "Of course, you know that any questions relating to race are not permitted." Nevertheless, some questions related to race were asked during interviews in which some of the deans did not get the position for which they were being interviewed. One of the deans, who was turned down for a dean's position prior to obtaining his current one, was asked by the president of an almost all-white institution why he, the candidate, did not like Black people. The president suggested that the candidate was "trying to get away from them [Blacks]." One dean was asked a question that a number of Black presidents reported that they had been asked: "Could I deal with faculty on a predominantly white campus?" Another Black candidate was asked during the interview for a dean's position for which he was not selected why he wanted "to move into a community where minorities are rare?"

None of the deans responding to the BS were asked questions relating to race when being interviewed for their current positions, suggesting that perhaps any questions relating to the subject had been asked and answered during the initial screening process. Without exceptions, their comments were positive regarding the interviews for their current positions. Some of their comments were as follows: "I do not think it [race] mattered." "I approached the interview as an academic individual. I tried to forget race during the process." "It [the attitude toward race] simply depended on the cultural maturity of the campus community." "Race was neither an asset nor a liability. I was a well-qualified candidate with a doctorate, three years of experience as a department head, an associate professor, three years of teaching experience in a large comprehensive community college, and 10 years of teaching and administrative experience in public schools." "It really didn't seem to be an issue in the interview process. I believe it was an issue in the actual decision-making process, but I was not involved in that. I had worked at the college for nearly 10 years before becoming dean. Interviews were with persons familiar to me." "The interview, as I recall, focused on gaining insight about my professional background, administrative style, decision-making skills, and my attitude toward students." And finally, "It [race] did not appear to be relevant."

Why were Black deans occasionally asked questions relating to race during interviews in which they did not get the position, yet were asked no such questions in the interviews that resulted in their being appointed to their current positions? One can only speculate. In the cases where they were turned down, it is conceivable that the interviews were conducted long enough in the past (one dean cited an interview he had in 1965 in which he was asked questions relating to race in regard to a position in the public schools in a Southern state) that questions relating to race were still being asked; or, the "fit" might not have been right from the perspective of those doing the interviewing and thus the candidate was pushed hard on certain points, including race; or, perhaps the candidates who lost the positions did a bit of healthy rationalizing and believe that race was an important factor in their not being selected. In any event, these are speculations and in no way excuse race ever entering an interview process unless it is understood by all concerned that the institution has special needs that might relate to the candidate's race.

While it is encouraging to find that race was not an issue for those Black deans who currently are deans of instruction, can one assume that race will not be an issue should these deans seek a presidency? Not necessarily, for they may find that race is a consideration in relationship to the type of presidency they are being considered to fill; therefore, they should be prepared to deal with the issue unemotionally, should it arise, especially if they are interested in becoming the president of a predominantly white institution in the suburbs.

Regarding the question of whether being Black helped in obtaining an interview, one female dean concludes that "being African-American and female was probably helpful." Another answered, "Yes, in a couple of interviews I was strongly recruited prior to public announcements of the position because I was Black, had a doctorate, and experience." From another: "Yes, I was included in at least one search process because I was Black. The college had no senior Black administrators." One dean who had been rejected by two institutions believes that being Black helped in obtaining an interview, but hedged a bit in his answer: "Probably. I felt this was true. The schools were both 95 percent white and had no Black faculty." Another dean was interviewed, he believes, because the institution wanted Black applicants: "The college was searching for Black applicants to meet EEO goals." One female dean points to the difficulty in determining what role, if any, race plays in the selection process. For example, she notes that, in the state in which she applied for and got a deanship, being Black was an asset because there were only two Black deans of instruction in the state. When she wanted to move to a different position with more responsibility, she believes that being Black assisted her in getting the interview. On the other hand, in another situation, she found that being Black and female might have hurt her chances for a position. Why? "The prior provost had been a Black female, and it was my perception that she had created an air of 'combustion' that probably was generalized to other Black females," she said. While she ultimately got the position she was seeking, her experiences illustrate the difficulty of determining when, or if, race is a factor in the selection process.

Three of the deans do not believe that race helped them in the interview process. One, who is dean at a historically Black institution, noted that his institution had no problem in getting a large pool of Black applicants for the deanship, especially since the search was an internal one with a large number of Blacks as applicants. Another, a Black female dean, answered that race did not aid her in the interview process because "I was urged to apply by my mentor, a white Jewish male." Another pointed out that it is not the policy of his institution to interview applicants because they are Black.

## ASSETS AND LIABILITIES

Are there assets and liabilities associated with being a Black and seeking to move into the top levels of community college leadership? If so, what are these assets and liabilities? Indeed, are the lines ever clear enough to determine whether one's race is an asset or a liability? Are Blacks ever included in the pool of applicants because of race? Before turning to the responses of Black deans to these questions, observations from a Black female dean help to place the questions in the broader perspective of community college leadership, especially in relationship to the self-imposed pressure to achieve excellence because other women and Blacks are watching and waiting for their own chance to lead. Her comments also serve to illustrate the complexity of being a woman, of being Black, of moving up the administrative hierarchy, and of taking the risk of moving over 1,500 miles to a new state and into a new position.

In my new position, I also find myself the only woman and the only Black at my level of administration, a fact that is unfortunately neither surprising nor uncommon. However, it is lonely. There are times when I feel I have no one with whom to share the day-to-day miseries without being perceived as inept (Wheelan, n.d., p. 5).

• • •

She described this feeling as "giving new meaning to the term 'triple threat' " for she wonders if that perception is based on her as a person, or as a woman, or as a Black. She continued:

But is there a difference in other people's perceptions of my skills because of my gender or my ethnicity? I can't answer that question without looking inside of myself and asking if I judge others along the same conditions. The reality is that often I do. No, it's not fair but it's human nature to judge others on the things by which they differ from you. For me, it's all right for people to judge me by my gender or ethnicity because I give all of my energies to ensure that I am being the best person I can be. For me, it is a motivating factor to think that I am a representative of other Black females. I am doubly determined to do my best because I am representing millions of others who do not have the same opportunity to demonstrate the fact that Blacks and females are competent, confident, determined, productive people too (Wheelan, n.d., p. 6).

• • •

## Perceived Assets

Again, a brief look at Black presidents sets the stage for examining Black deans. Ten of the 26 Black presidents responding to the survey identified their race as an asset in obtaining the presidency. Many of the assets identified by the Black presidents related to a specific institution or situation (the majority of the population was Black; the board was under the gun to employ a Black) and are likely not transferable into the larger realm of the community college leadership nationally. For example, one president noted that being Black was an asset because the college's student body was 70 percent Black, as was the city in which the college was located. Another noted that being Black was a major asset because only a Black person was going to be hired as president. Yet another refers to the board's affirmative action plan as a reason for his obtaining the presidency (Vaughan, 1989b, pp. 90–91).

The Black deans of instruction surveyed also were asked if being Black was an asset in obtaining their first dean's position. Their responses follow:

*The student body is overwhelmingly minority in make-up. No Black had been in the position of dean of faculty before.*

• • •

*Perhaps not in the ultimate selection, but all members of the college family are aware of the lack of inclusion of minorities in key positions.*

• • •

*Possibly. Currently the institution is under great pressure from the Board of Trustees and district president to hire qualified minorities.*

• • •

*I was 26 years old and a fairly bright kid. But that was not enough to be a dean in a small rural town. They needed to have a Black face to feel good about the one they had just run out of town.*

• • •

## Perceived Liabilities

Black presidents and deans were asked a number of questions regarding the relationship of race to their career. Of the 26 Black presidents responding to the question regarding the perceived liabilities associated with their race, only four saw being Black as a liability (12 of the 26 saw race as neither an asset nor a liability). These four saw such problems as an inability to break into the "old boys' network," being identified as Black, and the fear that they were viewed as "token" candidates (Vaughan, 1989b, pp. 90–91). The deans were asked if being Black was a liability in obtaining their first deanship. Their answers serve to illustrate that being Black still presents some problems for those individuals assuming positions of leadership in the community college.

One Black female dean believed that people in positions of authority had no confidence in her abilities and that she was a victim of covert racism. Moreover, being a minority and a female hindered her from becoming familiar with institutional politics, she believes. A Black male echoes a similar theme; he believes he suffered from the stereotyping of Blacks, being prejudged because of the color of his skin and because of inherent institutional racism. Another dean believes that he was rejected by two institutions simply because they were afraid of employing a Black dean. Another had a feeling of being a "token" and felt that he lacked credibility with his white colleagues.

Another Black dean found that because of his race, supervisors were unwilling to share information with him. Even his own self-confidence and professional posture presented some problems, often causing him to be labeled as aloof and uncooperative. He found that an obstacle on his way to the deanship was his own "lack of understanding of the necessity for Black administrators to respond to different issues with their ethnicity in mind." Another dean sees as a problem "convincing white faculty to address the special needs of students—often minority students—and teaching classes in a predominately Black neighborhood."

One Black female dean, whose career goal is to become a community college president, offers an interesting observation on what she perceives to be a potential liability facing her because of her race. "Raising funds for the foundation may be a problem. I don't know folks with the money, but they are white more often than not. I am always conscious of being both female and Black and asking (usually) white males for money. Probably irrational, but real."

As suggested in the introduction to this section, many institutions show no prejudices when employing personnel. For example, one dean reports that he experienced no difficulties on his way to the deanship because of his race. To the contrary, he "had the good fortune of being at two institutions with administrators who were very supportive." Another dean said that at first he "never took the initiative to apply and assert myself," factors that had nothing to do with his race.

The above observations come from an extremely small sample of Black deans. Nevertheless, faculty members, presidents, and trustees, as well as those Blacks aspiring to the deanship, should take the sampling as expressions of concern and be sensitive to the role race plays in the selection process for top community college administrators, for the above remarks serve to remind us that one's race can be perceived as a problem, even in advancing to the top leadership positions in "democracy's college."

## AFFIRMATIVE ACTION

Affirmative action programs provide the legal basis for assuring equal opportunity for all segments of society. Certainly community college leaders, both lay trustees and community college professionals, have been sensitive for a number of years to the need to consider minorities and women when employing deans and presidents. But has affirmative action had an impact on the community college professional?

Over one-half of the 26 Black presidents responding to the survey question regarding affirmative action stated that it aided them in becoming president. The ways in which they felt affirmative action aided their candidacy included: (1) being included in the pool of applicants; (2) sensitizing boards and others to the assets of Blacks; and (3) providing a general feeling throughout society that if the nation were to achieve its potential, then no members of society should be denied the opportunity to achieve their potential. One can summarize the Black presidents' views on the contribution of affirmative action as follows: affirmative action laws have kept the issue of equal employment opportunities before the public and therefore have caused those employing community college personnel to be more sensitive to the need to include minorities in the pool of applicants for all positions, including that of community college president (Vaughan, 1989b, p. 93).

Black deans also were asked on the BS if affirmative action aided them in obtaining the deanship. Five of the deans responding to the survey stated that affirmative action did aid them in becoming a dean. One dean, a highly respected national leader, pointed to the legal implications of affirmative action, citing the Adams case as a legal manifestation of the requirement that community colleges submit goals and timetables for meeting equal employment goals. Another dean notes that, while affirmative action probably did not influence her ultimate selection, "all members of the college family are aware of the lack of inclusion of minorities in key positions. The Office of Civil Rights keeps this issue before us." Another answered yes, affirmative action helped, "but only in an indirect way." One male dean with a Ph.D. in the sciences believes that affirmative action likely aided him "in getting the interview." Finally, one dean believes that affirmative action makes institutions sensitive to the need for diversity.

The conclusion regarding the influence of affirmative action on the employment of deans is essentially the same as on the employment of presidents: affirmative action has kept the issue of equal employment before the public and therefore aided the deans in being included in the pool of applicants for the deanship. The deans, as was true with the presidents, believe that they were well qualified for the positions for which they applied and that they would not have gotten those positions without the proper educational backgrounds and experiences, no matter what laws are on the books.

## MENTORS, ROLE MODELS, AND ASSOCIATIONS

As suggested above, minorities would seem to have a special obligation to serve as role models and mentors for members of their own race as well as for society in general. Again, as alluded to earlier, Black presidents pointed to the lack of being able to break into the network of peers as one problem in obtaining the presidency. The following is a brief look at the role mentors, role models, and peer networks play in preparing Blacks to assume the deanship.

## Mentors and Role Models

Six of the nine deans responding to the survey question on mentors stated that they had a mentor who influenced their careers. Only one of the deans pointed to a community college president as serving as his mentor. The most frequently mentioned mentor was a dean, with three pointing to deans as role models.

Over 38 percent (10 out of 26) of the Black presidents responding to the survey questions regarding mentors and role models stated that they had a mentor, two of whom were identified as being Black. The most common mentor was a community college president. Over 86 percent of the presidents stated that they had a role model who influenced their career, 12 of whom were Black (Vaughan, 1989b, pp. 94–95).

Seven out of eight deans stated that they had a role model who influenced their careers, two of whom also served as mentors. Of the six who had role models who were not their mentors, five had a Black role model. Although the sample is extremely small, Black deans, as is true with Black presidents, overwhelmingly choose members of their own race as role models, a situation that is not always possible in selecting one's mentor.

As more and more minority students enter the community college, serving as a mentor and role model will become increasingly important for minority presidents and deans. In many respects, the dean of instruction is in a better position than the president to fulfill these roles because of the contact the dean has with division chairs, faculty, and, to a lesser degree, students. Discussions with Black presidents and deans and observation of practices on a number of campuses reveal that the demands on Blacks in a predominantly white environment are overwhelming, thus leaving little time for mentoring. Institutional leaders might well forego the practice of placing a minority on essentially every search committee, on the affirmative action committee, and on almost every other college standing committee, if it means overburdening the minority professional to the extent that time for mentoring is eliminated. And, if the institution has a record of treating all applicants for professional positions without prejudice, Blacks certainly can be relieved of always having to serve on such committees, leaving time and energy for the all-important tasks of mentoring future leaders.

*Negative Role Models.* Deans and presidents were asked if they had a "negative role model" who influenced their careers. Eight (30 percent) of the Black presidents responding to the survey answered yes, and six of the eight "negative role models" were community college presidents. The "negative role models" often were autocratic or incompetent (Vaughan, 1989b, p. 95).

Two of the nine deans responding to the survey said that they had a "negative role model." In both instances, the "negative role models" were white but neither was a president. One found that the division director he worked for gave him "limited information about 'why' and instead just told me 'how'." This director also failed to correct him when he made an error and showed no support for his professional growth. The other dean had a "negative role model" who was unorganized, hard to get to see, gave no guidance, never gave a rationale for decisions, always waited until the last minute to perform tasks, had poor decision-making skills, and was poor at delegating tasks and responsibility to others.

Certainly pointing to such a small number of deans does little more than raise the issue of "negative role models." Nevertheless, deans, presidents, and other community college professionals should be sensitive to the need to project a positive image, for one never knows when one is being observed and serving as someone's "negative role model," a role few professionals desire to fulfill.

## Peer Networks and Non-professional Memberships

Four of the nine deans responding to the survey answered yes, they belonged to a peer group that aided them in becoming a dean, with one of the four identifying the peer group as being predominantly Black. Peer networks aided five of the 26 Black presidents responding to the survey and only one of the five belonged to a peer group comprised primarily of Blacks. One reason so few Black community college presidents belong to peer groups for Blacks is that so few exist (Vaughan, 1989b, p. 95).

Two Black deans indicated that non-professional organizations were important to their careers. Of the two, one listed membership on a state-level commission; the other listed contact with the governor of the state. As is well known, presidents have greater external responsibilities than do deans; nevertheless, minority deans should explore the desirability of cultivating more external contacts, an especially useful stance for those deans whose goal is to become a community college president. For example, in contrast to the Black deans, 18 of the Black presidents responding to the survey stated that external contacts aided them in their movement into the presidency, with eight of the 18 identifying more than one external group as being important. Black churches and the National Association for the Advancement of Colored People were the most popular organizations listed by the presidents. Only one Black president listed the Chamber of Commerce, a popular organization for community college presidents in general (Vaughan, 1989b, p. 96). Black deans who see few advantages in fulfilling their position resulting from their race should certainly see what doors, if any, their race opens in the community and use the opportunities provided by those doors to enhance their roles as deans and to help prepare for the next step in their careers, for the presidency requires community contacts and community activities to a much greater degree than is being practiced by the deans responding to the BS.

## Professional Associations

Ten of the Black presidents listed one or more professional associations that aided them in becoming a president. The most popular professional organizations among the presidents were the American Association of Community and Junior Colleges (AACJC), the Council on Black American Affairs, and the Black Presidents' Roundtable. No state organizations were listed by the Black presidents (Vaughan, 1989b, p. 96).

Four of the Black deans listed professional associations that aided them on their way to the deanship. Two listed the AACJC, one the American Association of Women in Community and Junior Colleges, and one the National Council on Black American Affairs. One dean, while noting that it was not an organized professional association that aided him, gained support from the administrators at another college. Based upon this extremely small sample, Black deans do not appear to have profited greatly from membership in professional associations. Nevertheless, those aspiring to the presidency should begin to build professional relationships that can assist them in obtaining their goal.

## Leadership Programs

Eleven of the 26 Black presidents noted that they had participated in a program to develop higher education leaders prior to becoming a president. The most popular program (listed by four of the presidents) was Harvard University's Institute of Educational Management (IEM) (Vaughan, 1989b, pp. 96–97).

One of the nine Black deans responding to the survey named previous participation in a leadership program (Leaders for the '80s) as important in obtaining the deanship. That more deans did not list more leadership programs might appear surprising on the surface. In reality, however, leadership programs such as Harvard's IEM and others tend to accept applicants who already are deans or above, especially when seeking participants from community colleges. Moreover, prior to becoming a dean, it is difficult for many individuals to receive the funding and to take the time away from the campus that is required to attend programs that range in length from two weeks, to five weeks (IEM), and even to one year (the American Council on Education Fellows Program).

## THE ARACIAL DEANSHIP

Kerr and Gade's statement regarding the asexual presidency was used as the basis for a question to determine if Black presidents and deans view their positions as aracial. Eighteen of the 26 Black presidents (over 69 percent) did not view the presidency as aracial. Prominent among the reasons given by the Black presidents for rejecting the presidency as aracial was that, when one is Black, a "double standard" exists whereby one is watched more closely and is expected to do more than one's white colleagues and is prejudged based on color rather than on qualifications (Vaughan, 1989b, pp. 97-98).

Six of the nine Black deans responding to the question on the BS rejected the deanship as being aracial. One dean noted that if one is "born Black, [one] is always perceived of as Black." He goes on to explain that, "I have never been in any administrative position where being Black was *not* an issue, particularly when faculty report directly to me." Similarly, from another: "I don't think any Black person ever feels that his/her Blackness is not considered by others when decisions are made. This is probably irrational and difficult to prove or deny; however, it is real." Another, a female dean, notes that, "Although my colleagues are cordial, I do not feel that my ideas are taken as seriously or that I am taken as seriously as my white male counterparts. My religious values are closely connected to my ethnicity and they are trivialized also." Another Black dean feels that a "damned-if-you-do-and-damned-if-you-don't" situation often exists: "There are expectations from Blacks that you perform in a way that will advance the [Black] cause. Others are observing to see whether or not you are being biased in your decisions." In the same light, another stated: "Sometimes, I feel that I am being observed more closely by faculty than other deans at other schools." Finally, from a Black dean who has been active in advocating more Black leadership in community colleges, comes the following:

*Racism is so pervasive in all institutions in the United States, and colleges and universities are not excluded. With few exceptions, most people (even the most liberal) see me and other African-Americans as Blacks first. They can't seem to get beyond race. I wish they could, because I see myself as a well-prepared professional who (through an accident of birth) is Black. I have many other virtues and talents, but if people see race first and foremost, then it is their loss.*

• • •

Some aspects of the dean's position are made more difficult because of race, some of the deans believe. One observes that, "Racism is a curious thing. My job is more difficult because I have to prove myself to my staff, my colleagues—especially the white males, and to the upper administration (some of them, at least). This is a continuous process, not proving myself once but over and over again." Another dean has been asked to serve on an inordinate number of community committees, and while he has enjoyed the service, "there is a tremendous time commitment which takes me away from my family. This situation could be resolved by an increased availability of Blacks in leadership roles with their organizations." Another dean believes that he has to be "better" than other administrators and that he has to "be open to students, support the faculty, be unbiased in my judgments, and still support Black issues." Finally: "Whenever I recommend another Black person who is competent, eyebrows are raised. I would be a fool to recommend someone who is incompetent."

Black deans, unlike Black presidents, perceive few advantages resulting from their race. For example, 12 of the 26 Black presidents found certain advantages; mentioned most often was that their race enhanced their ability to move among Black members of the community, a big advantage in communities and institutions where the majority of the population is Black (Vaughan, 1989b, pp. 99-101). In contrast to the Black presidents, not one dean stated that the dean's position was made easier because of race. As discussed earlier, one reason for the difference might be that presidents normally work more closely with the community than do deans; therefore, one would expect that being able to integrate themselves more easily into the community would be an advantage to which presidents would point, especially in those communities with large Black populations. On the other hand, one would think the Black deans would see some advantages not available to non-Blacks. For example, the perspective gained from being Black can be valuable in working with members of all races, something Black deans should realize and capitalize on.

## ADVICE FROM BLACK DEANS

The Black deans responding to the survey were asked what advice they would offer other Blacks who have the dean of instruction's position as a career goal. The following were among their responses.

*Know your discipline; know the institution; and know yourself.*

• • •

*Be prepared professionally by getting the doctorate; start in a faculty position and come up through the ranks if possible, for this will give you invaluable experience; develop a healthy self-concept by knowing and appreciating your roots; and do not depend upon reinforcement from others.*

• • •

*Attain the union card—the doctorate. Make friends with folks in a position to make calls, write letters, etc. on your behalf, regardless of their ethnicity. Remember to always be prepared to keep plugging away. Institutional fit may mean waiting for the most unlikely of places for a first assignment. Take it, prove yourself, then move to a place you really want.*

• • •

*Read, read, read. Engage in meaningful scholarly activities and research; involve yourself in your institution at all levels—students, faculty, staff, and administrators; participate in a variety of professional organizations and associations, thus learning from the success of others as well as to establish a network of diverse professionals.*

• • •

*Once you decide you want to be a dean, work, work, work for it.*

• • •

*Go to places or colleges that may not be personally suitable, but get the deanship for experience and professional mobility; develop your career carefully, and be academically well-grounded with teaching and administrative experience.*

• • •

*Lead, as much as practical, by consensus; base decisions and judgments on facts and reliable data.*

• • •

*If at first you don't succeed, try again; always strive for excellence.*

• • •

*Respond in a timely way to each request, even if the answer is no.*

• • •

The advice offered is sound in every case (and in most cases applies to all candidates, regardless of race) and taken in conjunction with the suggestions offered in Chapter 8, should give those individuals interested in becoming deans a good start on the pathway that will lead to the dean's office.

## THOSE WHO WANT TO BE PRESIDENT

Five of the Black deans responding to the BS stated that their career goal is to be a community college president. They were asked to list the three major obstacles to this goal resulting from their being Black. Two of the four identified obstacles they might face because they are Black. The other two listed obstacles that face most individuals interested in moving into a presidency, i.e., lack of experience in working with political groups, in fund rasing, and in finding the right institution, and few opportunities to observe the board-president relationship and to work more closely with legislators and community groups.

The two who saw potential obstacles resulting from their race noted such things as the location of the college, ethnicity of the student body, whether the institution is "culturally mature enough" to employ a Black, and, perhaps the most damaging of any comment, "withholding necessary opportunities and information preceding the application."

As the community college faces the future, the pathway to the presidency, while rarely easy, should nevertheless be open for more and more Black deans. The major problem is likely to be that there are not enough Blacks in the leadership pipeline to have a major impact on the make-up of the community college presidency in the foreseeable future, even in the unlikely event that every current Black dean of instruction assumed a presidency within the next four or five years. As one source notes, the number of Blacks entering teaching is decreasing as more and more Blacks seek better-paying jobs. "This has a negative effect on both the quality and quantity of the minority teaching pool. It also means that Black students will have far fewer role modes and mentors of their own race to help them achieve their educational goals" (Thomas and Hirsch, 1989, pp. 81–82). In regard to Black leadership at the top two levels, the challenge to the community college is twofold: (1) assure that current Black deans of instruction are encouraged and have every opportunity to become presidents; and (2) assure that the number of Black deans of instruction will increase significantly. Failure to meet these challenges will haunt the community college into the next century.

## SUMMARY

Blacks, who make up 10 percent of all community college students, appear to remain underrepresented in the leadership ranks of community college students. Indeed, only 3 percent of the respondents to my national survey of deans were Black. And despite a rigorous attempt to identify Black deans of instruction who could provide in-depth information on the Black experience in this important position, only 15 were located; of these only nine responded. Do these low figures accurately reflect the proportion of community college leaders who are Black? Until data on the ethnicity of college administrators are collected and reported at the national level, we can only speculate. But my findings tend to conclude that a shockingly low number of Blacks—surely less than 50—are on the traditional pathway to the presidency.

To be sure, community colleges are equal opportunity institutions, and for many of the Black deans who were interviewed, race was not an overriding issue in their professional advancement. The advice these deans have for other Blacks aspiring to the deanship is essentially aracial, stressing hard work, honesty, discipline, and other traits that are crucial to success in any professional endeavor, regardless of an individual's ethnicity. Yet for most of the Black deans, race was not an irrelevant factor. It manifested itself in the following ways:

- Some Black deans reported that they were asked questions about race during job interviews, at least during interviews for positions they did not obtain, despite the fact that such questions are usually illegal.

- While Black deans generally conceded that affirmative action has helped them indirectly by reinforcing the colleges' obligations to uphold equal opportunity hiring practices and assuring that minorities are included in applicant pools, several indicated that race was a liability in obtaining the deanship and in establishing credibility once the deanship was obtained.

• About half of the deans interviewed rejected the notion of the aracial deanship, noting that in some cases, race made it more difficult for them to carry out their jobs. Unlike the Black presidents (half of whom found certain advantages in being Black, especially in dealing with the Black community) *none* of the Black deans indicated that their race made their jobs easier in any way.

The problems raised by this small and admittedly unscientific sample of Black deans reflect the problems Black professionals face in American society generally and are not unique to the community college. Nonetheless, their comments are a reminder that while "democracy's colleges" do much to open higher education to Blacks and other minorities, we have not been as successful in increasing the ethnic diversity of our leadership ranks. Earlier, I made the case that today's deans look similar to today's presidents and that as a result, the profile of the presidency will not change greatly over the next decade or two. This is positive in many ways, lending continuity to a maturing but still growing segment of American higher education. It would be a shame, though, if this continuity extended to ethnicity, with Blacks and other minorities remaining underrepresented among those who are on the pathway to the presidency.

# 6

# *Hispanic Deans*

■

ispanics, as is true with most racial and ethnic minorities, are a
diverse group. One difficulty with determining how many Hispanics are in America is in defining the term Hispanic: are they
Cuban-Americans, Central and South Americans, Mexican
Americans, or Hispanics whose roots in this country pre-date Columbus?[1]

In an editorial titled "Hispanic Americans," the *Washington Post* (Sep-
tember 14, 1987), while noting that Hispanics are not a single homogene-
ous group, points out that in 1987 one out of 12 Americans was a Hispanic.
The *Post* notes that Hispanics in the United States tend to have relatively low education levels, with only a bare majority having finished high
school. The writer suggests that there are two ways to look at the plight
of Hispanics in America: "Hispanics tend to be behind other Americans,
to suffer from disadvantages; another [way of looking at them] is to say
that they are moving up rapidly, especially when you consider that many
started off living elsewhere, in circumstances you will not find statistically

---

[1]For a brief discussion of Hispanics and higher education see the chapter titled "Hispanics," by Gary
Orfield, in *Shaping Higher Education's Future: Demographic Realities and Opportunities, 1990–2000*, by
Arthur Levine and Associates, Jossey-Bass, 1989. Orfield examines demographic data on Hispanic
enrollment in U.S. schools and colleges from the 1960s through 1986–87. Two conclusions he reaches
are that in the future Hispanics will be the nation's largest minority and the segregation of Hispanic
students is intensifying.

replicated anywhere in the United States. Hispanics are moving up the many ladders of success in America" (p. A–18).

The community college has been a door of opportunity for those Americans who have for much of the nation's history found it difficult, if not impossible, to attend an institution of higher education. Expanding upon the editor's metaphor, one rung in the ladder of success for Hispanics is the community college. In 1987, approximately 354,000 Hispanics were enrolled in the nation's community colleges. This number surely will increase as the Hispanic population increases and as more and more Hispanics pursue higher education.

In 1985, 1.7 percent of all full-time faculty in the nation's institutions of higher education were Hispanic. When one considers that 55 percent of the Hispanics attending college are enrolled in community colleges, and 7 percent of the 5 million or so community college students are Hispanic, the picture facing these colleges and the nation becomes clear. If community colleges are to recruit, retain, and fully serve Hispanic students, more Hispanic faculty and administrators must be employed.

What does the paucity of Hispanic faculty members have to do with a discussion of Hispanic deans of instruction? The answer is obvious: the most important source of future community college administrators is from the faculty. Without Hispanic faculty in the pipeline, it will be virtually impossible for community colleges to increase the number of Hispanic deans and presidents. Without Hispanic deans and presidents, Hispanic students and faculty will be denied much needed role models and mentors, and the nation will be denied the many benefits that will result from their leadership.

As suggested earlier, it is very difficult to obtain information on Hispanic administrators. Indeed, a professional colleague who is Hispanic recently called me and discussed a study of Hispanic community college presidents he was contemplating. He had called a well-known researcher in higher education and was told that there were just not enough Hispanic presidents to justify a study. On one level, I agree with the researcher: data are limited and therefore any conclusions reached are tentative. On another level, I disagree: I believe we can learn much from the perceptions of Hispanic presidents, although the number is limited. The same is true of the perceptions of deans. Moreover, the choice is to ignore these important groups of leaders, certainly an unacceptable answer. With this in mind, the following reflects the perceptions of the 14 Hispanic deans who responded to the Hispanic Survey (HS) that was sent to Hispanic chief academic officers. When the Hispanic deans are compared with the Hispanic presidents, the information on the presidents is taken from my book, *Leadership in Transition* (Vaughan 1989b).

## MOVING INTO THE DEANSHIP

During the interview for the presidency, a minority of the Hispanic presidents experienced some questions that could be interpreted as having negative overtones; however, for the most part Hispanic presidents experienced no difficulty resulting from their ethnic background (Vaughan, 1989b, p. 102).

The deans responding to the HS were asked if being Hispanic helped them in obtaining an interview for the deanship and if any questions relating to their ethnicity were asked, either during the interview that resulted in their current position or during any previous interviews for the deanship.

Six of the 14 deans were turned down for a deanship prior to obtaining their current position. One of the 6 felt that his ethnic background played a role in his being turned down. His comments follow:

> I was once interviewed for a dean of instruction's position in which the board member (Anglo) began to speak to me in Spanish. I responded to him in Spanish. I asked whether this interview technique was being used for all finalists or if speaking in Spanish was a requirement. I was never given a clear answer. I have been turned down for several deans' positions and a few presidencies. On several of these I definitely feel that I was not given the position either because I was Hispanic or because I was single. Feelings are, however, most difficult to prove.

● ● ●

Another dean who was rejected for a position earlier in his career was asked some questions that he felt were not relevant to the position. He notes that, "The college president asked me how I would handle fellow Chicanos' concerns about my going up the 'ladder' of success. I found the question interesting, particularly because the college was 99 percent Anglo, both in employees and student enrollment."

The other four who were turned down for positions do not believe rejection resulted from their ethnicity. One candidate used the occasion of the interview to "re-direct a number of questions to enhance my candidacy through references to my multi-cultural and multi-lingual assets by linking them to the mission and purpose of the community college." Another candidate felt that her rejection resulted from being female, not Hispanic, for a Hispanic was chosen to fill the position for which she applied. Another candidate believes he was rejected for a position because he was too young, too inexperienced, and because his assertive stand on issues intimidated members of the committee.

Twelve of the 14 Hispanic deans responding to the HS commented on their ethnic backgrounds in relationship to being included in the pool of applicants for the deanship. One dean was included because, "The chancellor specifically was looking to balance the top staff with an Hispanic. Our local governing board is very ethnic conscious. Our local politics call for coalitions among ethnic communities; they are used for administrative appointments." Another dean answered yes, being Hispanic was a factor in obtaining an interview because the college had a student body of 24 percent Hispanic students but no Hispanic administrators. Another dean echoes a similar theme: "I know I have been granted an interview because they were seeking minority (Hispanic) candidates." From another: "Yes, the process strongly encouraged minority applicant consideration. Also, the president was very aware of the need for a minority higher-echelon administrator. The search committee was not just interested in an Hispanic but rather in minority representation." Another dean believes that being Hispanic "was a big factor. The college Hispanic student group had been getting more vocal about hiring Hispanic faculty and administrators. In addition, this particular college had been under pressure by Hispanic leaders and groups for not hiring Hispanic administrators." Another dean was even more adamant: "Absolutely. My current college is over 50 percent Hispanic in student enrollment. Being Puerto Rican and speaking Spanish were assets."

On the other side of the coin, three deans simply replied that, no, being Hispanic was not a factor in obtaining an interview. Four others rejected their ethnicity as a factor. From one: "I feel that my ethnic background had little to do with my selection when I was 28 or now that I am 42. What helped was knowing the people who were doing the hiring and the knowledge I could bring to the job." Another replied that being Hispanic was not a factor in getting the interview; indeed, he views it as just the opposite and that being Hispanic "precluded consideration for several positions." Another dean responded that, "No, being Hispanic was not a factor in most cases. I am sure that in a couple of cases I helped out someone's number game, but it was never a real consideration for the position." A female dean believes that being Hispanic "was an attractive characteristic, I'm sure, for EA/EO records but, in the final analysis, the choice is ruthless and insensitive to what you are. Once I was selected, I had to prove my selection every step of the way."

Another dean had his idealism shaken when he decided to move from a faculty position into an administrative position, and his comments illustrate some of the difficulties in attempting to determine what role one's race or ethnic background plays in the selection process.

> *I never wanted my ethnicity to be used as a 'crutch' that would open professional opportunities. I was somewhat naive to think that my employment credentials and experience would qualify me as a competitive applicant. WRONG assumption. I simply could not get interviewed. Then, when I obtained my doctorate and the chancellor encouraged me to become more visible by appointing me to district-wide committees, I was noticed by many other administrators.*

• • •

Were getting the doctorate and obtaining greater visibility the important factors in his obtaining the deanship? Or was his ethnicity the deciding factor, once the other factors came into play? The answer is not clear; nevertheless, it is an important question and one with which community college leaders, including governing boards, must struggle in the future.

Although four of the 14 Hispanic deans were asked questions that related to ethnicity, none of the questions appear to have been or were not perceived to be negative by those being interviewed. From one: "I was interviewed only by the chancellor who wanted to know about my commitment to the Hispanic community and how I would balance that with my overall commitment to the college." Another was simply asked if he spoke Spanish. Another also was asked about her "language abilities" and her past experience in working with a state-level office devoted to bilingual education. Another was asked how he would "provide leadership in meeting the needs of an increasingly diverse student population," certainly a legitimate question for any candidate for the deanship.

## OBSTACLES

Eleven of the 14 Hispanic deans responding to the survey felt they had encountered obstacles on their pathway to the deanship resulting from their ethnicity. Such comments as "faculty racism" and "institution-wide stereotyping" were used by one dean; another felt that if "too many Hispanics were in one place at the same time, the perception was that there were too many of 'them,' and some people had a difficult time perceiving me in a position other than menial." Another dean felt that he was never given an opportunity until a new president reorganized the institution. Another believes that the perception on campus was that he obtained the position "solely because of affirmative action," when in reality "external forces (Hispanics in influential positions)" played a major role in his being hired for the position. One Hispanic dean feels that he faced additional problems because he was expected to do more than others in the position, because he was "pigeon-holed as an Hispanic in student services," and that there was a "perception that [future] hiring would be influenced by the fact that I am Hispanic and might select others like me." From another: "There is a perception that ethnic staff are single-issue oriented toward ethnic issues and do not have the same general outlook as non-ethnic administrators." Similarly, from another, there is "an expectation that you will be 'one-dimensional,' i.e., will only see the Hispanic perspective." Another found that "without Hispanic representation in the administration, I found it difficult to 'join the exclusive old boys' club' of administrators. They didn't know me; I didn't know them."

One of the three female Hispanic deans responding to the survey saw her ethnicity as an advantage, but encountered obstacles because of her sex. "I believe the obstacles were more from being a woman than being Hispanic. The latter seems to have been an asset rather than an obstacle." As her response indicates, another female dean believes the obstacles she encountered ran the gamut since she was a female Hispanic in a technical field.

> Credibility: *I had none going in; even if they saw me 'walking on water' they wouldn't have believed their own eyes.* Gender: *Not only was I Hispanic but 'female' to boot! And I was in a technical field that was comprised primarily of white Anglo males whom I was to supervise.* Articulateness, intelligence, attractiveness: *It is a dangerous combination that threatens men or leads them to make grossly inaccurate assumptions about one's motives in questioning, discussing, etc.*

• • •

## AFFIRMATIVE ACTION

Hispanic presidents and deans were asked if affirmative action programs aided them in obtaining their positions. Only one president out of the 10 responding to the survey question indicated that affirmative action played any role in his obtaining the presidency. Therefore, I concluded that affirmative action programs have not played a major role in the selection of Hispanic presidents. Moreover, the perceived liabilities of being Hispanic and seeking a presidency were virtually nonexistent (Vaughan, 1989b, pp. 103–104).

On the other hand, nine of the 14 deans answered yes to the question regarding the role affirmative action played in their careers. While none of the deans believe that affirmative action programs alone were the reason they got their positions, a number believe the programs paved the way for their movement up the administrative ladder. Their views on affirmative action help in understanding the deanship as viewed from Hispanics: "Equal opportunity and representativeness requirements prevail over 'feeling comfortable' with the chosen candidate. [Affirmative action] is important to the image, recruitment, fund-raising, and overall community efforts of the college." "Programs do not make the difference: attitude, commitment to affirmative action programs is the key, and here the answer is yes." Other comments on the question of affirmative action included:

> When I applied for an assistant deanship at a New York college, they were looking for someone to supervise their off campus learning center, which had many Hispanic students enrolled. I was presented as the 'bilingual dean.' During the period when I was moving up the administrative ladder, there appeared to be an emphasis on hiring women and minorities. In point of fact, being a woman and Hispanic were real plusses in being named to a presidency as well, which has just happened.

• • •

> All applicants have an equal chance. There were 122 applicants for the position I am in now. No one can say I was given the position solely because I am Hispanic.

• • •

> An Hispanic was desired for my position.

• • •

> The president of the college was inclined to support affirmative action. This, plus a timely political climate in the community, made my candidacy much more pronounced and expedient. My credentials and experience were solid. These, and the fact that I'm Hispanic, gave me the edge over perhaps more published or nationally visible candidates.

• • •

*The chancellor and governing board had publicly committed to affirmative action. I am bilingual. In addition, I had worked in a community action program with a Chicano organization. I was also knowledgeable about the local community and schools and about the educational problems Chicano students were experiencing.*

• • •

*In California, A.B. 1725 has a very strong affirmative action component, and community colleges have been sensitive to the proposed legislative support long before the law was even adopted.*

• • •

*It's no secret that Chicanos/Latinos like me are few in number. With all the recent 'hoopla' about affirmative action, I have no problem making the group of final candidates for CEO positions. This is now; however, prior to the current affirmative action frenzy, I had difficulty getting interviewed.*

• • •

Three of the five who answered no, affirmative action did not aid them in obtaining the deanship, had comments. From one: "My skill as an administrator has always been a source of pride. Individuals have helped in getting jobs, but without my reputation as a mover and shaker and as a good manager, I would not have moved as fast as I have these past 12 years." Another noted that he has spent his entire professional career in education and that he hopes his "advancements have occurred because I'm good at what I do and it's recognized." From the third one: "No, I really feel qualified to do what I do. I just happen to be Hispanic."

## MENTORS AND ROLE MODELS

A lack of Hispanic mentors and role models was a problem for some Hispanic presidents (Vaughan, 1989b, p. 104). Ten of the Hispanic deans responding to the survey stated that they had a mentor who aided them in becoming a dean. With respect to ethnicity, three of the 10 had mentors who were Hispanic; two had mentors who were Black; one had a mentor who was white; and the ethnicity of the mentors of the remaining four respondents was not specified. In terms of gender, seven of the ten mentors were male; two were female; and one dean stated that he had more than one mentor, both female and male. The most popular mentors were individuals who occupied positions similar to the dean-ship to which the current deans earlier aspired; the second most popular mentor was the college president.

Mentors also serve as role models, but not always. Six of the 10 deans who had influential role models pointed to their mentor as filling the dual role of mentor-role model. One dean who stated that he had no mentor or role model who influenced his movement into the deanship illustrates the need for those in leadership positions to be sensitive to the various roles they play, including serving as a mentor or role model. His comment: "I was one of the 'first' and 'only'—a pioneer."

## Negative Role Models

While positive role models are important to minorities aspiring to the presidency or deanship, negative reinforcement also can be a factor in pushing one up the administrative hierarchy, if for no other reason than to "show them" that one is more capable of performing than is the other individual being observed. In an attempt to find if "negative rein-forcement" played a role in the careers of Hispanic deans, the survey asked these deans whether they had a "negative role model" who had built in them a desire to become a dean in order to do things differently from what they had observed. Twelve of the 14 Hispanic deans responding to the survey stated that they had "negative role models."

One current dean's negative role model was a former dean who was "paternalistic and patronizing." Another pointed to a former communi-ty college president who "was extremely competent in the technical sense but lacked the necessary human relations skills and empathy to gain wide-spread acceptance. This individual destroyed subordinates' dignity and morale, which ultimately led to an overall erosion of his support base." Another dean found his desire to succeed resulted from observing a presi-dent who was lazy, lacked integrity and a sense of pride and understand-ing in the community college mission. The president was, "in short, a clown! I realized I could do the job and be more effective." A female dean answered, yes, she had a negative role model: "He was my vice-president. He was illiterate, authoritarian, and had no social or interpersonal skills. He was an ineffective communicator and was threatened by me. He would not let himself be influenced by outside information. He was unilateral in his decision making. Have I said enough?" Another female dean also had her negative role models:

> Yes, two: one Hispanic male president who was not student-oriented and particularly did not attend to the needs of minorities, both students

*and staff. The second was a white male dean of the college (and previously my mentor) who is the most un-moral person I have ever met. In my path to the presidency, I have envisioned leading a community college as a humanistic community where people's needs are balanced against other factors, such as finances and regulations. I'm certain there is a better balance than what I have experienced in the college run by the two men described above.*

• • •

Finally, an eight-year veteran of the deanship places his experience with a negative role model in a light that illustrates the need for role models among members of racial and ethnic minority groups.

*For too long several Hispanics were chosen for key administrative positions because they were at the right place at the right time and the appropriate color (brown). The people represented a generation of Latinos who paid their dues but often never had the appropriate educational experiences or managerial history. For example, a president with whom I worked was selected by our chancellor because the chancellor needed a Hispanic with very strong faculty labor union affiliations. One problem: this Hispanic was a Spanish teacher with little administrative experience. After working for him just a few months, I knew he was overwhelmed and simply not prepared for this job. He certainly was a negative role model for me. Eventually he was asked to retire by our local board because of all the turmoil he had caused on campus. Chicanos-Latinos can no longer let this kind of story be repeated. We now have competent, qualified, educated, and trained Hispanics who are ready to be excellent role models for future Latinos.*

• • •

And finally, a bit of irony from a male dean: "I recently worked for a chancellor who motivated me through his *negative example*. In fact, this person has inspired me to not only want to become a college president but ultimately a chancellor of a multi-college district. I suppose I'll owe him a great deal some day!"

## PEER NETWORKS AND EXTERNAL CONTACTS

Only one of the 10 Hispanic presidents responding to the survey identified a peer network as aiding him in becoming a president (Vaughan,

1989b, p. 105). On the other hand, eight of the 14 deans responding to the survey indicated that a peer network aided them in becoming a dean. Two of the three female deans responding to the HS identified their peer network as predominantly female, although one also identified a peer group consisting of both males and females as influential in her development.

Eleven of the Hispanic deans identified community contacts as being important to their movement into the deanship. Among the organizations identified were the Latino Democratic Club, local Hispanic and other community organizations, and local Hispanic leaders. Only one dean mentioned often predominantly white male "mainstream organizations" such as the Chamber of Commerce, Rotary, and the Kiwanis Club, types of service clubs that are popular among community college presidents as a whole (Vaughan, 1986, pp. 24–25).

While peer networks and non-professional contacts appear to have helped Hispanic deans achieve the deanship more than similar organizations aided Hispanic presidents in moving into the presidency, the external contacts mentioned by the deans were overwhelmingly tied closely to their ethnicity and are contacts that are not as easily transportable to the national community college network as would be membership in national organizations such as the Rotary Club and Chamber of Commerce.

## PROFESSIONAL ASSOCIATIONS AND LEADERSHIP PROGRAMS

Eight of the Hispanic deans listed professional associations that helped them in becoming deans. Among the organizations listed (several of the deans listed more than one organization) were the American Association of Women in Community and Junior Colleges, which was mentioned by two of the women who responded to the survey; the AACJC, with two of the eight mentioning it; and the American Council on Education, with one mentioning it. Six of the eight mentioned state organizations that aided them in their movement into the deanship. None mentioned the National Community College Hispanic Council.

Three of the Hispanic deans identified national leadership programs that they had attended prior to becoming a dean. Two of the three, both of whom are women, identified the all-female Leaders for the '80s program as being significant in their development. (Indeed, one identified its leaders, Carolyn Desjardins and Mildred Bulpitt, as the grand champions of women in the community college.) One was an ACE Fellow. Two mentioned state workshops as helping their development.

## THE ARACIAL DEANSHIP

Of the 10 Hispanic presidents responding to the survey question, six believed the presidency to be aracial once they assumed the position. The four who do not feel that the position is aracial experienced some feeling of being under greater pressure to perform better than their non-minority counterparts (Vaughan, 1989b, pp. 106–107).

In contrast to the presidents, only two of the 14 Hispanic deans responding to the survey find the position to be aracial. Of the remaining 12, eight checked "no," the position is not aracial; one checked both "yes" and "no" in answering the question and provided comments on the question; two, both female, checked neither "yes" nor "no" but commented on the question; and one had question marks in both the "yes" and "no" boxes but commented on the question. Some of the comments regarding this question are enlightening and help to understand some of the frustrations experienced by Hispanic deans.

One of the deans who checked neither "yes" nor "no" had the following to say regarding the aracial nature of the dean's position: "It is very difficult to assess. People do not express racial attitudes directly toward me. I learn about them via third party dialogue and cannot always attest to their authenticity." The dean who checked both "yes" and "no" made the following comment: "Basically, yes, it is aracial, but one can never escape the inevitable scrutiny of co-workers who are ethnic minorities to see how 'you' will survive in a position traditionally not filled by minorities or women. There is an unwritten and unspoken pressure to succeed and to be even better than your predecessor." One of the three female deans who did not answer "yes" or "no" and who recently moved to a chief executive officer's position made the following comments that help one to understand and appreciate the dilemmas and pressures faced by a woman and ethnic minority dean.

*It's an interesting dilemma. I cannot disassociate myself from my gender or heritage just because I am a chief executive officer of a campus now. However, I have to make sure that my decision making is not perceived as 'pro-Hispanic' to the exclusion of others. I am so concerned that this is not happening that I often wonder if I'm not overcompensating at the expense of my Hispanic constituency. I have to watch where I step. I have to do what is right for all.*

• • •

A second female Hispanic dean, while believing the position to be aracial, comments on being a female dean: "I really don't believe being Hispanic has had an impact on my performance reviews; however, being a woman has made me more vulnerable to politically motivated attacks via my evaluations. I believe this very strongly."

Of the eight deans who answered, "no," the deanship is not aracial, one is female. Her comments relate to being a minority dean rather than to being a female dean, although she finds that being Hispanic often places her in the middle between members of her own ethnic group and others. Her response to the question of whether the dean's position is aracial, once there, follows:

> Absolutely not. We deal with resentment toward 'affirmative action,' fear of racial differences, and constant questions about our abilities and skills! On the other hand, we are questioned by our own people to see if we've been co-opted or at other times are expected to be 'super' human: role models, token board members, political activists, etc., in addition to our duties.

• • •

Another dean speaks of the pressure resulting from being in the middle: "There's a large Hispanic population in this community that is ever vigilant of my position and the role-model responsibility that it carries. While it is true that performance is the ultimate test, people are quick to resort to an ethnic-blame if the decision or outcome is unfavorable." Another dean speaks to the "superman syndrome." As a Hispanic, "You still have to be twice as good to be at a par with your Anglo counterparts. In most cases a Hispanic is not expected to succeed." Pressure from being Hispanic resulted for one dean because "It is assumed that all Hispanic CEOs are experts on what is bothering the Chicano community." One male Hispanic dean believes that for most people, positions at the president-dean levels are aracial, but he qualifies his response. He notes:

> There are some, however, who will never be comfortable with a leader who is not a white male. I have found that these people will usually manifest themselves one way or another, and I deal with them on a case-by-case basis. I try to project an attitude to them that I am 'good' and exactly where I should be. The problem is theirs, not mine. Fortunately, this latter group is a small minority—and my hope is that it's getting smaller.

• • •

Finally, one dean places the argument of whether his position is aracial in the larger context of society. His observations:

> This country has always had strong women in leadership positions. I don't, however, feel that the United States has had enough experience with minorities in leadership positions. I spent 10 years in Michigan prior to coming to California. (I've been here eight years now.) While in Michigan my administrative career path to higher positions was very quick paced. I've not found that to be the case in California, although I anticipate becoming a president within another year.
>
> I believe the difference for the phenomenon is that while in Michigan I was an anomaly—I was the only Hispanic dean in all of the 29 community colleges in Michigan. That is not the case in California. In Michigan, the Hispanic population is rather small in comparison to Blacks. I believe I posed no political threat to those in power in Michigan. In California, because of the heavy concentration of Hispanics, I believe I'm 'perceived' as a political threat by those who are responsible for decision making.

• • •

## ONCE IN OFFICE

The deans also were asked about their current positions and whether being Hispanic made their positions or some aspects of their positions easier or more difficult.

### Perceived Assets

Five of the Hispanic deans noted that there are aspects of the dean's position that are easier because they are Hispanic. All five noted that the major asset was in their ability to work with Hispanics. One dean believes that he has "a much more broad-minded view of the world and the many perspectives involved in analyzing situations and problems." Another believes that because she is Hispanic she is "more sensitive to some kinds of cross-cultural communications, and this has helped occasionally with student and staff problems."

### Perceived Liabilities

What difficulties did Hispanic deans experience once they assumed their deanship? Several of the deans noted that those characteristics of the position that keep it from being aracial are the same ones that cause difficulty in carrying out the duties associated with the position. Others had additional comments. One dean feels that there is an initial shock experienced by members of the college community who have never worked with people from different cultures and races. From another: "Too often college staff (faculty, in particular) cannot accept me as a Chicano administrator. They think the only reason I have this dean's position is because of my ancestry." One dean finds that being a dean makes it "more difficult to forcibly advance Hispanic issues, especially when the issue conflicts with Black or Asian issues." Similarly, from another dean: "Hiring of other minorities is scrutinized much more closely by all, including other Hispanics. [There is] a burden to always be well prepared so as not to 'look bad' in the eyes of the people who support you." Another dean finds the position more difficult because he is expected to be an expert on all Hispanic issues and because there are "expectations from Hispanic students and employees that the Chicano dean is going to make things 'right' for them."

## ADVICE FROM HISPANIC DEANS

The Hispanic deans responding to the survey were asked what advice they would offer other Hispanics who have the dean of instruction's position as a career goal. All 14 of the deans who responded to the survey offered advice. Most was sound advice for anyone seeking to move into a deanship and had little to do with being Hispanic and seeking the position. For example, future deans were advised to work hard, get the doctorate, be yourself, get a mentor, set goals, be honest and fair, take advantage of leadership workshops such as those offered by the League for Innovation and Harvard University, and know the instructional program. One dean, however, spoke directly to Hispanics aspiring to the deanship. Her advice:

> You must represent yourself as being broader than Hispanic; don't be a one-issue person. At the same time, you must demonstrate that your Hispanic background and language are added benefits. Don't refuse a position just because they are using you as a token; even as a token, you can still gain power and achieve things.

● ● ●

## THOSE WHO WANT TO BE PRESIDENT

Thirteen of the 14 Hispanic deans responding to the survey have the community college presidency as a career goal, although one of the 13 is a provost at a branch of a four-year university and currently considers himself a president; another former dean recently assumed a presidency. With respect to obstacles on the pathway to the presidency resulting from being Hispanic, three of the deans saw none. The other 10 saw some obstacles on their pathway, although not all are related to being Hispanic. For example, one dean sees being a single male as an obstacle; another needs to finish a doctorate; another considers himself to be too young; and another expresses uncertainty about how effective he would be as a president; all expressed concerns that apply to all individuals who seek to move into the presidency.

On the other hand, some comments regarding being Hispanic and seeking the presidency help to understand the deanship and the presidency. For example, one dean fears a lack of "acceptance of the idea of a Hispanic in the key leadership role." From a male dean: "I'm now trying to break into another exclusive club of old boys. Too often, I'm invited as a final candidate because boards and chancellors need to show that a brown face was considered. To obtain a CEO position I may have to relocate. Relocation would be traumatic." Another believes racial bias will hinder his movement into the presidency. Another believes the three obstacles in his way are, "Being Hispanic; Being Hispanic; and Being Hispanic."

Another dean fears "being seen as a single-issue person and facing a search committee that is prejudiced against minorities and truly wants the traditional white, middle-aged male." Further, he fears "seeking a presidency in a state or system that has already 'placed' the 'tokens' and really doesn't want any more minorities." Finally, a male dean fears that his "view of the world might be inordinately ethnic" and "consideration for a position could be limited to areas or searches heavily stressing minority representation." His conclusion: "[I fear] the perception that I might carry an ethnic banner that could color decision-making. A 'damned-if-you-do-and-damned-if-you-don't' dilemma."

## THE FUTURE

Can the community college meet the challenge of bringing more Hispanics into its top leadership positions? As is the case with Blacks, the pathway to the presidency must be open to Hispanic deans of instruction, and more of the deans must be encouraged to become presidents. The second challenge is assuring that more Hispanics are in the pipeline that leads the dean of instruction's position. If community colleges cannot meet these challenges, much of the nation's population will not be fully served by these colleges, for as one source notes, if current demographic trends continue, "Hispanic students will become the nation's largest minority group but at the same time will be highly disadvantaged educationally" (Orfield, 1989, p. 57). Certainly the challenge to community colleges is clear and formidable.

## SUMMARY

Hispanics, like Blacks, are grossly underrepresented in the community college's administrative ranks. Accounting for 7 percent of all community college students nationwide—and even greater proportions in the Southwest and other portions of the country—Hispanics made up less than 2 percent of the respondents to my national survey of deans of instruction. The seriousness of this underrepresentation is made even more obvious when one considers that 55 percent of all Hispanic college students attend community colleges, compared to 43 percent of all Black college students and 36 percent of all white college students. Despite the importance of community colleges to Hispanics, the survey results indicate that, as is the case with Blacks, a shockingly low number (perhaps as few as 20 or 25) are on the traditional path to the presidency.

The survey I conducted with 14 Hispanic deans provides grounds for hope and for concern. Hispanic deans reported that race played a sometimes negative role in their careers. Eleven of the 14 deans felt that they had encountered obstacles—including "faculty racism" and "institution-wide stereotyping"—on the way to the deanship as a result of their ethnicity. Most felt that the deanship was not aracial, noting that their status as minorities made them the target of resentment and placed a heavy burden on them to prove themselves or serve as role models. At the same time, however, the Hispanic deans were somewhat more likely than the Black deans to feel that affirmative action had helped in their careers and less likely to indicate that race played a negative role during job interviews. In addition, five of the Hispanic deans indicated that their ethnicity made at least some parts of their job easier, especially in dealing with a multi-cultural student body.

These are cursory observations drawn from an admittedly unscientific sample. The fact that the Hispanic respondents painted a somewhat more optimistic picture than the Black deans I surveyed should not mask the fact that community colleges have a long way to go before Hispanics are equitably represented among our top institutional leaders. The small number of Hispanic deans of instruction leaves us with the still-unanswered question: Where will tomorrow's Hispanic presidents come from?

# PART III

■

*The Ending*

art III of this volume is devoted to the more practical aspects of the deanship. Chapter 7 discusses the results of a leadership survey completed by those deans from across the nation who were identified by their peers as leaders within their respective states. The deans rank those personal characteristics and skills that they believe contribute to an individual being successful as a dean. Do the deans rank integrity above sound judgment? Is it more important to employ capable personnel or to communicate effectively? Or can one rank such basic aspects of leadership?

In Chapter 8 practical advice is offered on how future deans and future presidents can keep from "shooting themselves in the foot" when seeking to move up in the administrative hierarchy. This chapter is the most practical one in the book and should also aid board members in evaluating presidential candidates. This chapter contains advice from presidents and current deans on the "do's and don'ts" of seeking a new position.

The last chapter consists of a number of conclusions and recommendations, all of which grew out of the preceding chapters, yet are not simply a summary of what has been said. Rather, many of the recommendations are interpretative and may well cause some debate on the part of deans and presidents.

The final chapter also contains some messages from deans to presidents. What do deans want and expect from presidents? In this case, the deans are presented with a very rare opportunity when offering advice to presidents: they have the last word. A number of quotes by deans are used, most of which presidents should find enlightening, useful, and occasionally amusing.

# 7

# *Leadership*

■

I n an attempt to identify those deans of instruction who are viewed
as leaders by their peers, all deans receiving the CLS were asked to
name the two most effective deans in their state, excluding themselves. Any dean receiving three or more votes within a given state
was considered to be a leader in that state. The result was that 86 of
the 619 deans responding to the CLS met the minimum criteria and were
classified as leaders within their respective states. These 86 were then asked
to complete a dean's Leadership Survey (LS) [See Appendix 3]. Sixty-
three deans (73 percent response rate) from 31 different states responded
to the LS. The LS sent to the deans was almost identical to an earlier
survey sent to those community college presidents identified by their peers
as leaders within their respective states. The results of the presidential
LS provided the basis for the chapter on leadership in *The Community
College Presidency* (Vaughan, 1986, pp. 179–208). One reason for using
an almost identical survey for the deans and presidents was to be able
to compare the two groups in an attempt to understand both positions
more fully and to take a look at future community college presidents,
many of whom are currently deans of instruction.

## SIZE OF THE INSTITUTION

The deans identified as leaders serve at institutions that are larger (average size: 5,487 full-time enrollments [FTEs]) than the institutions of all deans answering the CLS survey (average size: 3,051); the median size of the institutions for the leaders is 3,725 FTEs versus 1,800 FTEs for the CLS deans as a whole. Only 12 percent of the deans identified as leaders are at institutions with fewer than 2,000 FTEs. It is clear that deans identified as leaders by their peers hold positions at the larger institutions.

Certainly outstanding leadership is not an inherent characteristic of serving in larger institutions; nevertheless, in many instances, larger institutions are often looked upon as the leaders within their respective states, commanding major amounts of the resources allocated to community colleges (one president identified as a leader led an institution that enrolled almost one-third of all community college students within the state; another president's institution enrolled almost half of all of the students in the state) resulting in greater visibility both within the state and nationally for the deans and presidents of these institutions. For example, those presidents identified as leaders by their peers also led larger institutions, with an average of 4,501 FTEs versus 2,030 for all presidents answering the presidential CLS (Vaughan, 1986, p. 197). Finally, all other things being equal, community colleges, like so much else in America, are often seen as better if they are bigger.

## NUMBER OF YEARS IN CURRENT POSITION

Size of the institution may be one factor in aiding a dean in achieving leadership status. Another factor is tenure in office. The deans identified as leaders had occupied their current position on the average of 8.7 years. The 8.7 years compares with an average tenure of 5.4 for all deans responding to the CLS. This author found in an earlier study that presidents identified as leaders by their peers also have been in their current positions longer (9.4 years) than the presidents who responded to the presidential CLS (5.3 years) (Vaughan, 1986, p. 198). Another study found that those presidents identified by their peers as the most effective presidents in the nation had held their positions approximately nine years (Roueche, Baker, & Rose, 1989, p. 74).

In the case of both deans and presidents, the tenure in office for those individuals identified as leaders far exceeds the five to seven years often considered to be the maximum time one can provide effective leadership in a given position. While one's effectiveness depends upon any number of factors, these figures indicate that community college leaders should evaluate many factors when considering how long is too long to remain in one particular position, for there is no magic number of years for providing effective leadership.

## AGE, SEX, RACE, AND ETHNICITY

The average age of the deans identified as leaders is 49.4 versus an average age of 48.3 for the deans as a whole who responded to the CLS. The median age for the deans identified as leaders is 49 years of age versus a median age of 48 for all deans. Sixty-six percent of the deans responding to the LS are between the ages of 46 and 55, with 1.6 percent under 40 years of age and 3.2 percent between the ages of 61 and 64 years of age.

Almost 86 percent of the deans identified as leaders are men and 14.3 percent are women. These percentages compare with the 79 percent of all deans responding to the CLS who are men and the 21 percent who are women. No attempt was made to compare the number of years female leaders had been in their current position with the number of years male leaders had been in theirs; nevertheless, a factor contributing to the smaller percentage of women identified as leaders versus the total number of female deans may be a result of tenure in office: the average number of years in current positions of the female deans responding to the WS is 3.6 years, versus the 8.7 years for the deans identified as leaders.

Of those deans identified as leaders by their peers, almost 97 percent are white, 1.6 percent are Hispanic, and 1.6 percent are Asian.

## MOBILITY

Fifty-seven percent of the deans identified as leaders live in the state in which they finished high school, versus 49 percent of the deans as a whole. The deans identified as leaders have held an average of 1.3 deans' positions versus an average of 1.6 for the deans as a whole. In contrast to the deans, presidents identified as leaders are more likely to have changed positions more often than have the presidents as a whole (Vaughan, 1986, p. 198).

## LEADERSHIP: PERSONAL ATTRIBUTES

Regardless of what theory of leadership one subscribes to, there are certain personal attributes associated with leaders. Those presidents identified as leaders were asked to rank the personal attributes they considered to be the most important for the effective community college president. The results were reported in *The Community College Presidency* (Vaughan, 1986, pp. 184–187).

Using that same listing of personal attributes, the deans of instruction who were identified as leaders were asked to rank the personal attributes of successful deans.

The rating scale used on the deans' survey of personal attributes ranged from 1 to 5, with a rating of 1 being of little importance and a rating of 5 being of extreme importance. The same scale was used in ranking skills and abilities of deans and of subordinates, both of which are discussed in the following pages.

### Ratings

The following discussion looks briefly at personal attributes that the deans identified as leaders consider most important versus those that presidents identified as leaders consider most important. The rankings of both groups are then summarized in Figures 1A and 1B.[1] In the discussion that follows, the deans' ranking is presented first, followed by the ranking of presidents. The presidential rankings are presented on a converted scale. The rankings should provide current and future leaders and governing board members with a yardstick by which to measure those personal characteristics required in the successful community college leader. The reader should keep in mind that deans and presidents consider all of the personal attributes important in the successful leader. Also, when the rankings are relatively high on the scale, the comparison between deans and presidents shows little actual difference between what the two groups consider to be important.

*Integrity.* The personal attribute receiving top ranking by deans was personal integrity, with almost all deans giving it the highest ranking. Presidents also ranked integrity at the top of the scale, although sound judgment received the same high ranking by presidents. Obviously, deans

---

[1]The presidential LS was based on a scale of 1 to 3, with 1 being of little importance and 3 being of extreme importance. Realizing that a 5-point survey is not a duplicate of a 3-point survey, nevertheless the presidential survey was converted to a 5-point scale in order that the rankings of the two groups can be more readily compared.

and presidents agree that the basis upon which sound leadership should rest is the personal integrity of the leader.

*Judgment.* The personal attribute receiving the second-highest rating by deans is the ability to exercise sound judgment. As noted above, sound judgment tied with integrity as the top-ranked personal attribute on the presidents' scale. Not surprisingly, then, deans and presidents agree that the successful community college leader must exercise common sense in making ethical decisions.

*Commitment to the Community College Philosophy.* The deans of instruction ranked commitment to the community college philosophy third, whereas the presidents ranked it sixth.

*Courage to Make Difficult Decisions.* The deans ranked courage fourth; presidents ranked it third. In both cases, courage to make difficult decisions is viewed by both deans and presidents as a mandatory characteristic of the effective leader.

*Loyalty to the Institution.* Ranking fifth on the deans' scale and seventh on the presidents' scale was loyalty to the individual institution.

*Concern for Others.* The sixth-ranked personal attribute on the deans' scale was concern for others. Presidents ranked concern for others fourth. While both groups ranked concern for others high, one might find it somewhat surprising that presidents ranked it higher than deans since deans have more daily contact with more members of the college community than do presidents. On the other hand, presidents may view the entire institution as the mechanism for enhancing the well-being of others and consider the president as the symbol of the institution and thus responsible for the well-being of all individuals associated with the institution.

*Flexibility.* Ranked seventh by the deans and fifth by the presidents was flexibility. The relative rankings make sense in that presidents tend to have more flexibility to make decisions than do deans, who often must reflect the decisions of presidents. Nevertheless, the deans view flexibility as an extremely important personal characteristic.

*Drive or High Energy Level.* Ranking eighth by both the deans and presidents was the need for the successful leader to have a high level of physical and intellectual energy, which is translated into the drive to accomplish the requirements of their respective positions.

*Willingness to Take Risks.* Deans ranked the willingness to take risks ninth, a category that was not included on the president's survey.

*Sense of Humor.* The deans ranked a sense of humor tenth whereas the presidents ranked it eleventh.

*High Intelligence.* The deans ranked high intelligence tenth; presidents ranked it fourteenth. While both groups ranked intelligence high (deans,

Of Extreme Importance          5.00

                                          Integrity (4.92)
                                          Judgment (4.92)

                                          Courage (4.70)
                                          Concern (4.60)

                                4.50

                                          Flexibility (4.34)
                                          Philosophy (4.30)
                                          Loyalty (4.24)
                                          Energy Level (4.14)
                                          Optimism (4.10)
                                          Excel (4.08)

                                4.00

                                          Humor (3.84)
                                          Health (3.72)

                                3.50

                                          Ambiguity (3.36)
                                          Intelligence (3.32)
                                          Social Ease (3.28)
                                          Curiosity (3.12)

Of Considerable Importance     3.00

                                          Charisma (2.96)

Of Little Importance           1.00

**Figure 1A:** Relative mean ratings of personal attributes for presidents.

Of Extreme Importance          5.00

                                         Integrity (4.83)
Judgment (4.68)
Philosophy (4.57)
Courage (4.56)

                               4.50

Loyalty (4.41)
Concern (4.40)
Flexibility (4.27)
Energy Level (4.02)

                               4.00

Risks (4.00)[1]
Humor (3.89)
Intelligence (3.86)
Optimism (3.86)
Excel (3.81)
Ambiguity (3.71)
Health (3.54)

                               3.50

Curiosity (3.48)
Social Ease (3.48)
Charism (3.06)

Of Considerable Importance     3.00

Of Little Importance           1.00

**Figure 1B:** Relative mean ratings of personal attributes for deans.

[1]Not included on presidents survey.

3.86; presidents, 3.32) it is clear that, relatively speaking, neither group places high intelligence among the top personal attributes. One would assume that both groups take a certain level of intelligence for granted when evaluating the requisites for the top leaders in an educational institution.

*Optimism.* Ranking twelfth on the deans' scale was optimism, whereas presidents ranked it ninth.

*Desire to Excel.* The deans gave the desire to excel a ranking of thirteenth, whereas the presidents ranked it tenth.

*Tolerance for Ambiguity.* Ranked fourteenth by the deans and thirteenth by the presidents, the tolerance for ambiguity received a relatively low ranking considering the nature of the two positions. (Keep in mind, as illustrated in Figures 1A and 1B, none of the personal attributes received low mean ratings.) Indeed, tolerance for ambiguity often makes the list of leadership characteristics required of leaders in all walks of life.

*Physically Healthy.* The deans ranked physical health fifteenth and the presidents ranked it twelfth. As with intelligence, it is likely that both groups take for granted that the person occupying the position is healthy enough to perform the requirements of that position.

*Curiosity.* Ranking sixteenth on the deans' list and sixteenth on the presidents' list is intellectual curiosity, a low ranking relatively speaking but a characteristic still considered to be important by both groups.

*At Ease in Different Social Situations.* Seventeenth on the deans' list is the ability to be at ease in different social situations. The presidents ranked this characteristic fifteenth, a relatively low ranking considering the number of different social situations presidents find themselves in. It is conceivable that by the time a person reaches the dean's or president's level, he or she has faced any number of different social situations and no longer finds new ones a challenge.

*Charisma.* On the bottom of both the deans' and presidents' lists as a desirable personal characteristic is charisma. The low relative ranking may be because charisma has become something of a cliche in American society, conjuring images of JFK, white horses, and Camelot, images most presidents and deans have difficulty identifying with. Even so, deans gave charisma a 3.06 and presidents a 2.96 mean rating, thereby not discounting it as a desirable characteristic for those occupying the positions.

In the "Other" category, deans listed personal characteristics that tended to overlap with the ones discussed above. For example, one listed "be a self-starter;" another "common sense;" another "loyalty to the president;" and another "ability to get along with others." Certainly any list of personal characteristics would include many of the ones discussed above as well as others one might add. For example, if I were repeating the survey for presidents, I would include the willingness to take risks as a separate category on the presidents' list. The list, however, is not intended to be all-inclusive; rather, it represents an attempt to determine which personal characteristics community college deans and presidents view as important in achieving success in their positions.

Developing a ranking of personal characteristics raises some interesting questions. For example, can judgment be taught? If so, how and by whom? Are values (integrity) formed largely during one's youth? Or is there value in having a course on ethics included in graduate programs designed to educate future community college leaders? Also, there is certainly some cross-over between what is an innate characteristic and an acquired skill. For example, is risk-taking something someone does automatically or is it a skill one develops after learning when to hedge one's bets, risking only what one can afford to lose? And how many of the personal attributes discussed above should the outstanding leader possess? All? The top 10? Certainly no one can say with certainty. I do believe, however, that no community college leader can long succeed unless he or she possesses the top-ranked personal attributes of integrity and sound judgment. Without them, the foundation is weak and other attributes lose much of their meaning. For example, a person who is quite flexible but who has low integrity and poor judgment is doomed to failure. The same case can be made for many of the other personal attributes discussed above.

## LEADERSHIP: SKILLS AND ABILITIES

Effective leadership in today's community colleges consists of more than personal attributes. The effective dean or president must possess a number of skills and abilities, of which the demand may change as one changes positions or as circumstances change. For example, the ability to process and manage information, while always important to those in positions of leadership, continues to increase in importance as the nation and the world move increasingly into the "information age."

Those presidents identified as leaders by their peers were asked to rank the skills and abilities they consider to be most important to the effective community college president. As was the case with personal attributes, the results of the ranking of skills and abilities were reported in The Community College Presidency (Vaughan, 1986, pp. 188–191). Using the same listing of skills and attributes that were used in the presidential

LS, deans of instruction identified as leaders were asked to rank the skills and abilities they considered important to the effective dean of instruction.

## Rankings

The following brief discussion compares the rankings of the deans with those of the presidents, with the deans' rankings coming first. The same 5-point scale and conversion from a 3-point scale to a 5-point scale for the presidents' rankings that was used in the discussion of personal attributes is used in the discussion of skills and abilities. With two exceptions, all of the skills and abilities were ranked either of extreme or of considerable importance. The rankings are summarized in Figures 2A and 2B.

*Select Capable People.* The deans of instruction ranked the ability to select capable people as the number one ability required of the successful dean. The presidents ranked it a very close second (4.86) to their top-ranked ability to produce results, which had a 4.92 ranking.

*Communicate Effectively.* Deans ranked the ability to communicate effectively as the second-ranked skill required of the successful dean of instruction, whereas presidents ranked it fourth.

*Ability to Analyze, Synthesize, and Evaluate.* Third on the deans' list was the ability to evaluate, analyze, and synthesize information needed in the dean's role. The presidents ranked this ability number six on their list.

*Produce Results.* Ranked fourth on the deans' list was the ability to produce results, the number-one-ranked ability on the presidents' list.

*Resolve Conflicts.* Deans ranked the ability to resolve conflicts among members of the college community fifth on the list of skills and abilities, whereas presidents ranked it third.

*Motivate Others.* Number six on the deans' list was the ability to motivate others; presidents ranked this ability fifth.

*Work as a Member of the Team.* The deans ranked the ability to work as a team member number seven; presidents ranked it twelfth, although it was still of considerable importance. In reality, it is often necessary for the president to step back from the team in a way that deans are not expected to, especially in their relationship with presidents.

*Relate to a Broad Range of People.* Deans ranked the ability to relate to a broad range of people eighth on their list; presidents also ranked it eighth on their list.

*Communicate the College's Mission.* Deans see the ability to communicate the college's mission and needs as the number nine priority, whereas presidents ranked it seventh.

*Define Problems and Offer Solutions.* Ranked tenth by the deans and ninth by the presidents is the ability to identify and define problems and to offer solutions to these problems.

*Perceive and Take Opportunities.* Deans ranked the ability to see and take opportunities as they occur eleventh on their list; presidents ranked it tenth.

*Process and Manage Information.* The deans ranked this skill twelfth; presidents ranked it fifteenth. The relatively lower mean ranking given by presidents might imply that they rely on others, including deans, to process and manage much information before it reaches the president's office.

*Community Understanding.* Deans ranked understanding the community and region the institution serves thirteenth. Presidents gave it an identical ranking, which may be a bit surprising since one would think presidents would place greater emphasis on understanding the community than would deans, especially considering the external aspects of the presidency.

*Performing Independently.* The deans ranked the ability to carry out duties and develop programs without supervision fourteenth on their list of skills and abilities; presidents ranked it fifteenth.

*Delegation.* Delegation of authority and responsibility was ranked fifteenth by the deans; the presidents ranked it eleventh, a lower ranking than one might expect considering the chief executive officer's position.

*Maintaining a Peer Network.* Next to the bottom of the deans' list but still considered important (3.26 mean rating) is establishing and maintaining a network of peers. Presidents also ranked it next to last and gave it a mean rating of 2.96, indicating that they feel it is relatively unimportant for presidents to maintain a network of peers. The low ranking of the importance of peer networks enforces the provincial nature of the community college, especially in the case of presidents.

*Produce Scholarly Publications.* At the bottom of both the deans' and presidents' lists of desirable skills and abilities is the ability to produce scholarly publications. The deans gave it a mean ranking of 2.21; the presidents gave it one of 1.56. Their ranking, while not surprising to those individuals who understand the community college's rejection of research in favor of teaching, does little to enhance the image of the community college as an institution of higher education devoted to the pursuit of truth and knowledge through any number of avenues.

## SKILLS AND ABILITIES OF SUBORDINATES

Both deans and presidents were asked to use the same list and the same scale to rank those skills and abilities they see as important in their

Of Extreme Importance    5.00

Produce Results (4.92)
Select People (4.86)
Resolve Conflicts (4.70)
Communications (4.68)
Motivate Others (4.58)
Analyze, Evaluate (4.54)
Articulation (4.54)
Relate (4.52)

4.50

Define Problems
  and Solutions (4.38)
Take Risks (4.22)
Delegation (4.16)
Team Player (4.04)

4.00    Know Community (4.00)

3.50    Manage Information (3.50)

Independence (3.22)

Of Considerable Importance    3.00

Peer Network (2.96)

Publications (1.56)

Of Little Importance    1.00

**Figure 2A:** Relative mean ratings of president's skills and abilities.

| | | |
|---|---|---|
| Of Extreme Importance | 5.00 | |
| | | Select People (4.58) |
| | 4.50 | Communications Skills (4.50) |
| | | Analyze and Evaluate (4.42) |
| | | Produce Results (4.39) |
| | | Resolve Conflicts (4.36) |
| | | Motivate Others (4.36) |
| | | Team Player (4.32) |
| | | Relate (4.26) |
| | | Articulation (4.21) |
| | | Define Problems and |
| | |    Solutions (4.19) |
| | 4.00 | |
| | | Take Risks (3.95) |
| | | Manage Information (3.94) |
| | | Know Community (3.89) |
| | | Independence (3.87) |
| | | Delegation (3.86) |
| | 3.50 | |
| | | Peer Network (3.26) |
| Of Considerable Importance | 3.00 | |
| | | Publications (2.21) |
| Of Little Importance | 1.00 | |

**Figure 2B:** Relative mean ratings of dean's skills and abilities.

subordinates. Rather than deal with each item separately as was done above, the following summary points out those areas that deans view as more or less important for subordinates than for themselves. Figures 3A and 3B provide summaries of how deans and presidents rank the desired skills and abilities of subordinates and may be used to compare and contrast the various views.

## Deans' Views of Subordinates

The deans' top-ranked ability for subordinates is to work as a team member, whereas they ranked it number seven on their own list of desirable abilities. Not surprisingly, presidents ranked the ability to work as a team member high (second) on their list of abilities they desire in subordinates (it was thirteenth on their own list of desirable abilities for presidents), subordinates who include deans of instruction. The conclusion is clear: those in charge believe it is more important for subordinates to participate as team members than it is for themselves to do so. This is the case whether they are deans or presidents.

On the other hand, deans view the ability of subordinates to produce results, to select capable people and to communicate effectively in the top five rankings for both themselves and their subordinates.

Interestingly, the deans rank the ability to define problems and produce solutions number four for subordinates and number 10 for themselves. Similarly, presidents also rank this ability fourth for subordinates but ninth for themselves. As is the case with wanting subordinates who are team members, both deans and presidents feel it is more important to have subordinates who can define problems and offer solutions than it is to be able to do so themselves.

Other minor differences can be seen from examining Table 1. It is also worth noting that deans and presidents agree on the bottom two skills and abilities desired in subordinates: both groups rank the ability to establish and maintain a network of peers sixteenth and the ability to produce scholarly publications seventeenth.

As is the case with personal attributes, any list of skills and abilities required of the successful community college leader is somewhat arbitrary and certainly incomplete. On the other hand, by ranking skills and abilities for themselves and for their subordinates, deans and presidents offer some signposts that might be useful in selecting community college leaders in the future. Moreover, a ranking of skills and abilities provides benchmarks for deans and presidents as they evaluate their own performances and those of their subordinates.

# RELATIONSHIPS

The deans responding to the CLS were asked to describe their primary relationship with faculty, subordinates, and students. In each case, the respondents were asked to check only the principal role, or if what they considered to be the principal role was not listed, to list that role. The responses provide yet another perspective on the dean's position.

## Faculty

Two-thirds of the deans responding to the LS stated that their principal role with the faculty is that of educational leader. Listed a far-distant second, with 14 percent of the responses, was the role of articulating the college's mission and serving as an advocate for that mission. Next was that of overall faculty supervisor (nearly 8 percent); any number of "other" roles (nearly 5 percent); symbol of the college (nearly 5 percent); and role model (nearly 2 percent). Not a single dean listed colleague as the principal role they play in relationship to the faculty, nor did any dean list the role of mentor to the faculty as the principal role, certainly putting to rest the myth that deans are really faculty members at heart.

## Subordinates

Over 24 percent of the deans identify their principal role in relationship to those individuals who report to them as that of articulating the college's mission and serving as an advocate for that mission. A close second is serving the role of motivating subordinates (almost 23 percent); the next principal role is that of colleague (16 percent); next, supervisor (13 percent); mentor (almost 10 percent); role model (6.5 percent); and "other" (6.5 percent). An encouraging sign for future community college leadership is that over 16 percent of the deans view their principal role in relationship to their subordinates as that of mentor or role model and another 16 percent identify it as colleague, which, in the best of all worlds, takes on many of the characteristics of mentor and role model. The differences in the way the deans view their roles in relationship to faculty versus subordinates indicates that deans may not have as close a relationship with faculty as might be the case in the highly romantic version of academia where administrators are considered "first among equals." Moreover, considering the number of deans and presidents who have degrees in education and who have built their careers on moving through the administrative ranks rather than on scholarship in a discipline, it is not only idealistic but unrealistic to view administrators as "faculty members on temporary assignments." Indeed, I argued in *The Community College*

Of Extreme Importance    5.00

                              Produce Results (4.92)
                              Team Member (4.74)
                              Resolve Conflicts (4.70)
                              Define Problems
                                and Solutions (4.58)


                         4.50

                              Analyze, Evaluate (4.48)
                              Motivate Others (4.48)
                              Select People (4.48)
                              Communications (4.36)
                              Manage Information (4.10)
                              Relate (4.10)
                         4.00 Articulation (4.00)


                              Take Risks (3.84)
                              Delegation (3.66)
                              Know Community (3.62)
                              Independence (3.60)

                         3.50




Of Considerable Importance  3.00

                              Peer Network (2.96)


                              Publications (1.50)

Of Little Importance     1.00

**Figure 3A:** Relative mean ratings of president's subordinate, skills and
     abilities.

Of Extreme Importance     5.00

            Team Member (4.52)

            4.50

            Produce Results (4.32)
            Select People (4.24)
            Define Problems and
              Solutions (4.19)
            Communications Skills (4.16)
            Resolve Conflicts (4.16)
            Analyze and Evaluate (4.15)
            Motivate Others (4.15)
            Relate (4.11)

            4.00

            Take Risks (3.94)
            Independence (3.94)
            Articulation (3.90)
            Manage Information (3.84)
            Know Community (3.66)

            3.50

            Delegation (3.45)
            Peer Network (3.13)

Of Considerable Importance   3.00

            Publications (2.11)

Of Little Importance       1.00

**Figure 3B:** Relative mean ratings of skills and abilities for dean
        subordinates.

| Skill/Ability | For Deans | For Subordinates |
|---|---|---|
| Analyze and Evaluate | 4.42 | 4.15 |
| Articulation | 4.21 | 3.90 |
| Communications Skills | 4.50 | 4.16 |
| Define Problems and Solutions | 4.19 | 4.19 |
| Delegation | 3.86 | 3.45 |
| Independence | 3.87 | 3.94 |
| Know Community | 3.89 | 3.66 |
| Manage Information | 3.94 | 3.84 |
| Motivate Others | 4.36 | 4.15 |
| Peer Network | 3.26 | 3.13 |
| Produce Results | 4.39 | 4.32 |
| Publications | 2.21 | 2.11 |
| Relate | 4.26 | 4.11 |
| Resolve Conflicts | 4.36 | 4.16 |
| Select People | 4.58 | 4.24 |
| Take Risks | 3.95 | 3.94 |
| Team Player | 4.32 | 4.52 |

**Table 1:** Comparison of mean ratings of skills and abilities for deans and their subordinates

*Presidency* (Vaughan, 1986) that once most individuals assume their first administrative position—division chair, for example—they change professions as well as job assignments (p. 45).

### Students

As discussed earlier, a number of deans take great pride and satisfaction in helping students achieve their goals. At the same time, the deans admit that they rarely work directly with students. What, then, are the principal roles of the deans of instruction in relationship to students? Over 36 percent of the deans view their major role as being the individual who communicates the college's mission and standards to the students. Thirty percent of the deans see their principal role as demonstrating to the students that they, as deans, are interested, concerned adults devoted to the welfare of students. Nineteen percent view their role as a symbol of authority; and over 14 percent listed a number of "other" roles as their major role in relationship to students, including providing inspiration and serving as ombudsman for students in academic matters. Not one of the deans listed "role model" as the principal role of the dean in relation to students. Based upon their perceived relationships with students, deans are correct in recognizing that their satisfactions obtained from student achievement, must, for the most part, be gained vicariously.

## RISKS AND WORKLOAD OF THE DEANSHIP

The deans were asked on the survey about the risks involved in serving in a deanship and the workload that deans face. Their responses should help to answer questions that those interested in securing a deanship might have.

### Risks

Those presidents identified as leaders by their peers were asked if they considered the presidency to be a low-risk, moderate-risk, or high-risk position. Thirty percent of the presidents responded that they feel the presidency is a high-risk position; 68 percent view it as a moderate-risk position; and only one president of the 63 presidents answering the question views the position as low-risk (Vaughan, 1986, p. 211).[2]

Of the 62 deans responding to the question on the LS, almost 52 percent view the deanship as a high-risk position; over 43 percent view it as a moderate-risk position; and almost 5 percent view it as low-risk.

While the deans were not asked to comment on the risks inherent in the deanship, a few did. One veteran dean's comments (this individual has served as dean under seven different presidents, in each case reporting directly to the president) help in understanding why he views the position as high-risk.

*In most cases, the dean fills the "second-in-command" role within the community college. By that nature alone, the individual occupies a high-risk position for two major and contrasting reasons. One reason is*

---

[2]The spouses of the presidents identified as leaders were asked for their perceptions of the risk associated with the presidency. Forty-two percent of the spouses returning the survey view the presidency as a high-risk position; 55 percent view it as a moderate-risk position; and 3 percent as a low-risk position (Vaughan, 1986, p. 212). The spouses of deans of instruction were not surveyed for this study.

*because of the threat implied to the president. The dean is the target for problems within the college even more so than the president, even more so today than yesterday. Yet the dean does not enjoy any security within the organization. Add to this the need to handle problems and issues with only the implied power of the presidency rather than the actual power, and the role becomes extremely creative and high-risk. The second reason is also because of the threat to the president. The deanship is high-risk because of the visibility of the role of internal leader, or at least leader of the faculty. If successful in a transformational leadership role, that can be a serious threat to the perceived image and fragile ego of the president. Very few presidents can handle a strong dean in a leadership role, particularly at the community college. As a result, the dean may back off from the transformational or even symbolic leadership role within the college, emphasize the transactional role, or seek other employment. Of significance too is the fact that most deans are upwardly mobile and desire a presidential opportunity at some point in their careers. The president of the college wherein the dean is now employed holds the reins on that individual's future. The president can be of enormous help in placement of the dean for a presidency, or can ruin the individual's professional career and profoundly affect that person's life.*

● ● ●

## Workload

Almost 94 percent of the deans responding to the LS view the dean's workload as heavy. The remaining deans view it as average, with none of the deans responding that their workload is light. One dean believes that the workload is "much heavier than the president's." Another feels that the workload is "almost beyond the point of endurance"; another considers it "very heavy, but that it seems light when you enjoy your work."

Without doubt, most effective deans of instruction work hard and long hours. When the heavy workload is coupled with the risks inherent in the position, the deanship seems an unlikely position for the lazy or timid. On the other hand, the position is at the crossroads of much that is happening at the institution. So, in spite of the risks and work associated with the position, most deans seem to enjoy their roles immensely. In the next chapter, a number of deans comment on why they would recommend the deanship to others, in spite of what some people might see as negative aspects of the position. Before moving to the next chapter, however, a challenge is issued to those deans who expect to lead the nation's community colleges into the future.

# SCHOLARSHIP: LEADERSHIP'S UNANSWERED CHALLENGE

Anyone reading this volume who is unfamiliar with the community college will surely be puzzled and perhaps even shocked by the deans' bottom-of-the-scale ranking of the ability to produce scholarly publications, both for themselves and their subordinates. How, the stranger at the community college's door will ask, can an institution's chief academic officer fail to place a higher value upon scholarship? Even those individuals who understand and are devoted to the community college may question the low ranking assigned scholarly publications by the deans.

Do deans place little value on scholarship, or just view publications resulting from scholarly activities as relatively unimportant? If community colleges have failed to emphasize scholarship, why has this been the case? Are there new and pressing reasons why deans should pay more attention to scholarship in the future than they have done in the past? What can deans, as leaders, do to enhance their image as academic leaders? Is scholarship the leadership challenge deans have failed to answer? The following examines these questions and makes recommendations regarding the dean's role as scholar and promoter of scholarship.

## Scholarship and the Community College

The LS survey contained the following statement: "Historically, community college professionals (faculty and administrators) have devoted little time to scholarship." The deans were then asked if they agreed or disagreed with the statement and why they agreed or disagreed. Over 95 percent of the deans responding to the LS either fully or partially agreed with the statement. The answers as to why community college professionals devote so little time and energy to scholarship varied, although most of the comments revolved around the following four themes.

*The Community College as a Teaching Institution.* A major theme centered around the feeling that since the community college is a teaching institution, community college professionals are not expected to devote any great amount of energy or time to scholarship. One dean who believes that scholarship has been neglected in favor of teaching warns that "The danger is that community college professionals will not stay in touch with the world around them, especially their discipline." Another dean, failing to make the connection between scholarship and teaching, suggests that scholarship has been neglected "because we are primarily practitioners and doers and have little time for the research and reflection necessary for scholarship." Another dean echoes a similar theme: "Our focus has been on teaching and learning and on creating an atmosphere in which the interaction between student and teacher is maximized." Finally, "Historically, we have created a dichotomy between time spent on scholarship and time spent on teaching and have focused our efforts on time spent on teaching. Given the choice between expending efforts on teaching or doing scholarly research, we have opted for teaching," one dean said. The teaching versus scholarship theme has definitely played a major role in the attitudes of community college professionals toward scholarship.

*Lack of Rewards.* A second theme expressed by the deans was that since faculty and administrators are not required to engage in scholarship, there have been very few rewards for doing so. As one dean notes, "It [scholarship] is not often a consideration in job performance evaluations." Another dean states bluntly that whether one engages in scholarship or not has no effect on gaining tenure. Yet another dean expresses the lack of incentives for doing scholarly work. His comments: "The community college reward systems do not recognize scholarly contributions as a significant aspect of faculty and staff remuneration." Finally, scholarship "hasn't been valued and rewarded organizationally; indeed, it has been suspect!" Most busy professionals expect to be rewarded for the time and energy they devote to their professions. In the case of scholarship, a number of deans responding to the LS do not perceive any great number of external rewards resulting from engaging in scholarship, either for themselves or for the faculty.

*Lack of Time.* Time, or the lack of it, was the third theme that emerged as hindering the community college professional's willingness and ability to engage in scholarship. Indeed, a lack of time resulting from heavy workloads was given as the single most dominant reason why community college professionals neglect scholarship. As one dean notes: "[There is] not enough time to devote to scholarship. There are just too many responsibilities, so scholarship takes a low priority." Another dean acknowledges that the "12–15-credit teaching load" leaves little time for scholarship. Several other deans refer to the heavy workloads for both faculty and administrators and to the lack of resources available for scholarship. A lack of time, coupled with a lack of rewards, can certainly impede scholarly activities and must be seen as major obstacles to the community college devoting more time to scholarship in the future.

*The Historical Setting.* The last theme to be discussed is perhaps the most important: the historical development of the community college. This theme, in many ways, encompasses the other themes, for a lack of emphasis on scholarship in its historical development would cause community colleges to fail to devote time, energy, resources, and rewards to scholarship; and, certainly the historical theme encompasses the commitment to teaching. One dean notes that "the community college in its infancy had and some continue to have an identity crisis. Unlike universities with their long-standing traditions and formal rituals, the community college sought a unique identity and many rejected the traditions research universities hand out." The dean does not endorse the community college's approach, however, for he notes that "scholarship is the core of our profession. Not to encourage it is to intellectually starve and wither away. The problem is to find ways to fund the paradigm shift." Another dean, noting the neglect of scholarship in the community college's past, refers to the lack of a historical commitment to scholarship: "Community colleges have spent their early years defining their roles, accommodating growth, and little focus has been given to the number one quality control in community colleges: top quality faculty in every position." Yet another notes that "as community colleges were established the focus was on buildings, staffing, curriculum development and rapidly growing enrollments" and not on scholarship. From another: "The teaching, service, and results-oriented approach that is a part of the institutional culture does not promote a value for scholarship..." Another dean notes that community colleges have historically focused on the day-to-day management of the institution and on "putting out brush fires." As a result, community colleges have put "less focus on academic leadership." One dean believes that "the real reason for a lack of emphasis [on scholarship] was that the community college movement was not recognized as a separate profession but as an extension of either the public school or university systems." And from another dean comes the following observation: "Historically, our institutions placed greater emphasis on processing students through the institution toward or into a career. Greater emphasis was placed upon skills than upon creative or intellectual pursuits." And from another comes the observation that "Much of this attitude [toward scholarship] is derived from the old two-year college philosophy which said that two-year colleges are teaching institutions, not research institutions. This attitude has (and is) costing us dearly." The community college's youth, rapid growth, search for identity, independence, and pragmatic nature all contributed to a history that did not lend itself to scholarship in the traditional sense of the term.

## Changes in the Wind

Does the lack of emphasis on scholarship accurately describe the situation today and in the future? Not necessarily, according to a number of the deans responding to the LS. Forty-nine of the deans responding to the LS believe that there are forces interacting with the community college that are calling attention to the need for more scholarship. Nine deans do not agree that there is a new awareness of the role of scholarship in relationship to the community college. The remaining respondents (5 deans) either did not respond to the question or gave a "maybe" answer. The new awareness of scholarship comes from a number of sources but, as is the case with the reasons for a lack of emphasis on scholarship in the past, can be grouped around central themes. I have identified three.

*Maturing of the Community College.* A major theme indicating that community colleges should devote more time and energy to scholarship is the maturing of the community college. One dean captures the essence of this argument well: "The new awareness comes with maturity of the community college. We can now look back and see that there are classic academic traditions that transcend time and [institutional] culture. This does not mean a biology professor in a community college needs to conduct basic research. It does require that every professional keep up with his discipline and engage in appropriate scholarship that will make him a better classroom teacher." Another dean notes that "as the community colleges mature there is less emphasis on accommodating growth and more on improving quality; scholarship and quality go hand in hand." Similarly, from another dean, "Community colleges are now on their feet, and they have recognized that the world changes. We need to change also, but more important, *lead* change." Another dean points to a "new confidence" because "community college professionals no longer have a sense of themselves as second-class citizens. There is now a sense of being full partners in the higher education enterprise, partners who have something to say to their colleagues." On the same theme, one dean notes that today "Community colleges are more clearly considered a part of higher education, and we are beginning to 'imitate' our senior colleges!" Other comments refer to the need for the community college to acknowledge more fully its role as an institution of higher education.

*Evaluation and Accountability.* Especially important in the thinking of those deans who would like to see more emphasis placed on scholarship is the concept of linking research to classroom activities, or "classroom research," as the concept is popularly known. "Classroom research" is seen by a number of deans as a means of improving teaching and making community college professionals more responsible for the teaching and learning process.

One dean, who agrees that there is a new awareness on the role of scholarship in the community college but who does not feel that it has been neglected in the past, offers his views on the subject: "I agree that there is a new awareness. The focus on scholarship has simply been intensified in the recent past. This intensity I view as a natural result of nationwide concern for reform in education and of nationwide acknowledgement that the community college is the vanguard and most effective mechanism to date for bringing true positive effects urged by education reform." Another dean notes that "various external and internal factors" are causing considerable discussion on the effectiveness of community colleges; therefore, "the need for scholarship is more critical and more apparent." Another dean notes the "shifting from quantity to quality" and that the "increased accountability for student outcomes" has increased the need for scholarship in the community college.

The pragmatic nature of the community college, which some deans feel has been an impediment to scholarship, is viewed by others as a reason for engaging in scholarship. From one dean: "The rise of 'applied research' generally and its increased legitimization in the academic community has helped community college folks feel that it may be appropriate even in the pragmatic, non-esoteric culture" of the community college to engage in scholarship. Another dean, drawing on the community college's programmatic nature, refers to the "strong perception that good decisions, planning, futuring, are based on sound data and sound understandings. Scholarship is one means to knowing, theorizing, projecting, and testing hypotheses." Similarly, another dean notes that "As a practitioner, I am interested in how problems are solved and challenges met in other institutions." Another dean combines the pragmatic with the philosophical: he believes that community colleges now have "the need to have some solid base for what we do, a scholarly basis rather than it just feels right; community colleges are coming of age. Of a more negative nature, community colleges are experiencing more criticism and must be able to respond, to defend." Similarly, a dean suggests that "some defensiveness has arisen [on the part of community colleges] as 'outsiders' have begun to study community college education." He offers the most pragmatic argument of all: "If we don't take responsibility for scholarship, someone will do it for us."

*Faculty Renewal.* A third theme, though less pronounced than the other two, is the need for an aging faculty and administration to find new avenues of renewal, of which scholarship may be one. One dean observes that "leaders of the 1980s and 1990s have spent most, if not all, of their professional careers at community colleges. These educational leaders do not expect to 'move up' to four-year colleges. When they do research it will often be on what they know best: the community college." From another dean: "Ignoring scholarship has helped to lead to burn-out and stagnation." Another dean points to the "graying of the professorate" and the resulting need for "personal and professional revitalization." Another dean sees scholarship as a means of "motivating teachers who have been at it for over 20 years." Finally, one dean believes that there is "a higher level of individual now working at the community college" and that this type of individual is aware of the connection between the scholar and the community college educator. Moreover, he contends that faculty are exploring a variety of ways to present their subject matter, resulting in an increased emphasis on professional development through scholarship. Finally, one dean believes that community college faculty "cannot remain on the cutting edge of their profession unless they maintain an active interest in scholarship."

## Answering the Challenge: Bringing Scholarship to the Forefront

Many deans who are viewed as leaders in their field endorse placing more emphasis upon scholarship. As the institution's academic leader, no one on campus is in a better position than are deans of instruction to make scholarship an integral part of the community college's philosophy and ultimately its mission. As the leader of the faculty, no one on campus is in a better position than are deans of instruction to provide the leadership in creating a climate on campus that includes a renewed commitment to scholarship. In essence, no one on campus is in a better position to answer leadership's unanswered challenge of making the connection between scholarship and outstanding teaching, thereby increasing the effectiveness of the community college in serving its students.

## Defining Scholarship

Scholarship on the community college campus (and on most other campuses, for that matter) is a concept in search of a definition, for rarely have deans, presidents, and others within the community college ranks even discussed a definition of scholarship, much less agreed on one. One result is that answers to a question regarding scholarship rely too heavily on the respondent's concept of what constitutes scholarly activities. One of the deans responding to the LS discusses the lack of a definition: "The difficulty, however, in responding to this question is caused by the fact that 'scholarship' can mean different things to different people. Are we talking about scholarship as applied to faculty, students, others? I hope that in the community colleges we never give up our interaction with students or our involvement with the learning process, so that we can have time to produce 'useless' research that might enhance our careers but not add much to our knowledge and understanding."

A first step in making scholarship an integral part of the community college philosophy is for deans and others to agree upon a definition of what they mean when they refer to scholarship. After much consultation with scholars in a number of fields, I developed the following definition of scholarship which, I believe, offers a good starting point for defining the term in a way that is in concert with the community college philosophy.

> Scholarship is the systematic pursuit of a topic, an objective, rational inquiry that involves critical analysis. It requires the precise observation, organization, and recording of information in the search for truth and order. Scholarship is the umbrella under which research falls, for research is but one form of scholarship. Scholarship results in a product that is shared with others and that is subject to the criticism of individuals qualified to judge the product. This product may take the form of a book review, an annotated bibliography, a lecture, a review of existing research on a topic, a speech that is a synthesis of the thinking on a topic. Scholarship requires that one have a solid foundation in one's professional field and that one keep up with the developments in that field (Vaughan, 1988, p. 27).

• • •

Implied, but not stated in the above definition, is that scholarship can also take the form of any number of traditional publications, including books and articles, that results from one's scholarship but not necessarily one's research. The definition is compatible with the community college as an institution devoted primarily to teaching and fits well with the community college philosophy, I believe.

A second step the deans of instruction can take is to have their national organization, the National Council of Instructional Administrators, endorse the pursuit of scholarship as a worthy and necessary undertaking for the nation's community colleges. Included as a part of the endorsement should be the recognition that the institution's chief academic officer will provide the leadership locally and nationally that will result in scholarship being included as a part of the community college mission. The time is right for the deans of instruction to make such a move, for they can build upon the strong call for scholarship contained in the 1988 report of the AACJC Commission on the Future of Community Colleges entitled *Building Communities: A Vision for a New Century* (pp. 25–28). For the deans to fail to capitalize on the Commission's report is to miss a rare opportunity that is so tailor-made for any group of community college leaders below the president's level to make a significant and lasting impact on the community college's philosophy at both the local and national levels.

Third, the deans of instruction, through their national organizations, should publicize what they are doing on the local campus to recognize and promote scholarship. Those deans responding to the LS provided outstanding examples of how scholarship is recognized on their own campuses, with deans taking the leadership role.

Finally, and most importantly, deans of instruction should assume the leadership on their own campuses to help the college community define scholarship, to have the college community endorse the definition and the activities required to accomplish the definition, and to recognize and promote scholarship on their own campus. Included as a part of the leadership role is demonstrating in any number of ways the vital link between scholarship and outstanding teaching.

By assuming the leadership role in making scholarship an integral part of the community college mission, the deans will emerge as truly academic leaders. The result will be that the unanswered challenge will have been answered: scholarship will finally occupy a place of prominence in the community college's philosophy and on each campus. The most logical group among the nation's community college leaders to answer the unanswered challenge would be the deans of instruction. To ignore the challenge is to fail to grasp that rare moment in history when a group of leaders can make a significant and long-lasting difference in how the community college views itself and how it is viewed by others.

# 8

# Advice for Those Who Would be Deans and Presidents

■

Of the 619 deans responding to the CLS, almost 55 percent stated that becoming a community college president was their career goal. Assuming deans responding to the CLS are representative of deans as a whole, one can conclude that of the approximately 1,169 chief academic officers serving the nation's community colleges, well over 500 of them aspire to become community college presidents. The number of individuals aspiring to the deanship is not known, but one would assume that the number is equally as impressive. The following advice is based upon personal judgment and the judgment of deans and presidents, upon my own experiences as a dean and as a president, upon my studies of the community college presidency, and upon the foregoing discussion of the dean of instruction.[1]

---

[1]Portions of the following were published in *Leadership in Transition: The Community College Presidency* by George B. Vaughan. ©1989 in the ACE/Macmillan Series on Higher Education by Macmillan Publishing Co., reproduced by permission of the publisher. The material has been altered somewhat and adapted to the current discussion.

# PREPARATION

Anyone who has read this far should have a good indication of some of the requirements for the dean of instruction's position. Chapters 2 and 3 discuss the backgrounds of current deans, backgrounds that should enlighten anyone interested in becoming a dean. The chapters on women, Blacks, and Hispanics discuss some special problems and opportunities faced by members of these groups as they move up the administrative ladder. These chapters also make a number of points that all potential presidents and deans should take to heart.

In addition to the material already covered, a number of deans were asked what advice they would give those individuals who aspire to the deanship. The following quotes make some points that are best made by someone currently serving as a dean. They also provide the basis for my own advice for those who aspire to the deanship and to the presidency.

### Deans' Advice on Preparing for the Deanship

One veteran dean who has held three successful deanships offers the following advice: "First of all, get some training for the job. By that I mean a good, sound academic background. Second, I think the person ought to serve a journeymanship in the classroom, know what teaching and learning is about, and be able to carry that flavor into the relationship with the faculty before aspiring to a leadership role. Now I'm assuming some leadership ability, the ability to relate to people well, and all of that." From another dean: "I think the individual should gain as much experience as possible, taking on a variety of different tasks and volunteering for those tasks. I would advise that you get some academic preparation in educational administration, for while I do not think there is any substitute for learning on the job, I think there are some shortcuts that can be achieved by academic work. I think that [those who wish to become a dean] need to really consider how they work with other people on campus, establishing relationships, and to understand that every relationship is going to have some impact on the future of the deanship."

A female dean suggests, "Be visible. Make a speech *every* chance you get; it is wonderful for increasing confidence." Similarly, from another female dean: "Prepare well. Complete the appropriate degree (earn the doctorate) and serve as the leader of campus-wide committees; participate widely in leadership of professional organizations." Another dean, who had only been in the position for two years at the time of the interview, offers his advice to aspiring deans: "I think the young person who's interested in eventually being a dean of instruction needs to understand that the primary path—and I think it's the best path—to the deanship is through the academic ranks. I recommend that the individual get a master's degree in a teaching discipline and spend some time teaching in the community college; spend some time as an assistant division chair or department head until an opportunity arises to move into the division chair's position. Do that for three to five years, and I think the person is ready."

One dean who has served in every administrative position on campus but "college business manager and president," [nor has any desire to serve in either position] believes that basic to any preparation for the deanship is the desire to become a dean. Once that is decided, individuals must realize that they build upon "the skills they learned in the last job." He notes that the future dean must communicate well, both in writing and verbally. Finally, "The other piece of advice is never to underestimate the value of any person you have out there. Use them, not in the fact of using them, but use them as a part of the institution to make it better."

One female dean whose husband supported her as she moved up the career ladder, even to the extent of being a househusband for an extended period of time, offers this advice: "I believe very strongly that we should not be consumed by the mental challenges of a position and that our health, spirituality, and social needs are equally important, and I don't think you function well unless you keep that balance well." One dean admonishes those who have the deanship as a career goal to take advantage of every opportunity available, including those "not normally at the campus level but at the regional and national levels. I think developing a network of colleagues is absolutely critical for a variety of reasons. That network can help you deal with problems, come up with solutions, give you the names of individuals who can help you. Get to know more individuals outside of your sector, outside of your region even, and utilize that talent that's out there." One chief academic officer, who was a director of continuing education prior to assuming the deanship, advises the future dean to become familiar with the literature on leadership and management in higher education, while at the same time keeping abreast of the national trends affecting the academic scene. As he states it: "Know what the trends are so that you can provide direction on campus."

One female dean believes that many community college leaders view the community college's comprehensive mission too narrowly. Her advice to the future dean: "Don't be narrow. Look at the issues from a variety of perspectives. Get involved in the community. Continue with your interests. Be a whole person; don't get too focused on the job." She has taken her own advice, for she relates the following: "I've taken a lot of time in the last couple of years to think about leadership and to avail myself of every opportunity to talk with other people from around the country and from a variety of institutions—community organizations—and to really think about the issues. I urge all deans to do the same thing, to think about leadership as an issue, to grapple with it on a personal and a professional level. Engage in the struggle: that would be my advice."

One veteran dean keeps his advice short and to the point: "Find a successful dean and try to model after him/her. Understand what it takes to function as a leader and a manager and understand the difference between leading and managing." Similarly, from another dean: "Study in detail the way your president makes decisions and work to gain his/her trust in your assessment of proposed actions." Finally, from another dean: "Know that the 'best' person doesn't exist among candidates in a pool, only the 'right' person at a particular moment."

## Common-Sense Approach to Preparing for the Deanship and the Presidency

Much of the advice offered by deans and presidents can be summarized under a number of categories, most of them based upon experience and common sense. The following actions and considerations, while in no way guaranteeing anyone a deanship or a presidency, should aid interested individuals in evaluating their potential and making preparation for joining the ranks of community college top leaders. With the caveat that not all of the advice and observations apply equally to those aspiring to the deanship and the presidency (for example, those who aspire to the deanship should ignore much of the advice relating to governing boards, at least until they are successful deans and aspire to the presidency), the advice is nevertheless a common sense approach to applying for most professional positions, including the deanship and the presidency.

*Earn a Doctorate.* This is basic advice offered by practically every president and dean with whom I have discussed the subject. Without the doctorate, a candidate's chances of becoming a president or dean will be greatly diminished and indeed eliminated in many cases. One president, when asked about the pathway to the presidency, responded that the "doctorate is, in many cases, the key to the executive washroom. It's considered minimum." A dean suggests that if you want to be a dean, "Get the terminal degree (even if it means making sacrifices) so you will be taken seriously." While it is not a universal rule that one must have the doctorate to become a dean or even a president, the fact remains that most presidencies and many deanships today require the doctorate.

Nevertheless, some would-be presidents and deans continue to dream that they will be the exception to the rule. For example, in a state with over 20 community colleges and a community college system with a 25-year history during which no one ever served as a president who did not have the earned doctorate, a dean without the doctorate was deeply hurt because he was not even considered for a recent presidential vacancy. With an increasing number of doctorates granted each year, governing boards do not have to, and few will, consider candidates without the doctorate. In many cases, the same applies to deans. In any event, the person with the doctorate will likely be selected for a deanship or presidency, all other things being equal.

*Secure a Position in a Community College.* The primary audience for which much of this volume is intended is already "playing in the right game," for approximately 90 percent of the community college presidents come from within the community college ranks, a percentage that has increased over the years and may become even higher in the future. The number of deans coming from outside the community college field is so small that it is not even worthwhile for most individuals to contemplate moving directly into the deanship from outside the community college field. The point is that it is very difficult to obtain one of the community college's top positions from outside the community college field.

*Get into the Academic Pipeline.* While one can make it to the presidency and deanship (as pointed out earlier, deans have followed any number of pathways to the deanship) through routes other than the academic one, the odds of becoming a dean and especially a president (the pathway to the presidency narrows considerably and focuses upon the academic dean's position as the jumping off point) increase if the academic path is followed, a point that is emphasized a number of times in the advice offered by deans for future deans and in *The Community College Presidency* (Vaughan, 1986) in relationship to the presidency. Future deans and presidents should note that more and more search committees and governing boards require that presidents possess teaching experience. A successful president of a large community college in the East provides a useful perspective on teaching, the deanship, and the presidency. His advice: "I know that the short-cut has been not to bother to teach for many younger presidents. I think that's a mistake. I really would encourage some teaching experience, full-time, not just part-time. I think my 9 years of teaching before I became a dean were critical to my development." A dean suggests that if your goal is to become a dean, it is best to "move up through the ranks—teacher, division chair, dean—for the best understanding of the role. And remain in a line position, not staff." The academic pipeline, then, is from the classroom, to division chair, to dean of instruction, to president.

*View the College from a Broad Perspective.* Never say "It isn't my problem because I'm only concerned with instructional matters or financial matters or student services." As one dean observes above, "Don't be narrow" in your thinking. For example, many student services professionals make the mistake of saying over and over that they are "student-oriented." Who isn't? Be college-oriented while at the same time presenting the perspective of your division. Future deans especially need to think in terms of the college as a whole for, as was pointed out in Chapter 3, many deans found their perspective too narrow upon assuming the deanship.

*Find a Good Mentor.* In an interview I conducted with Edmund J. Gleazer, Jr., former president of the AACJC, he offered the following advice. "Find two or three good mentors. You will find that there are some key people in the field; make it a point to get to know them. Try to get into the network; go to work for well-known and competent people if you can. A good president will employ good people and will provide the opportunity for those people to achieve their own visibility." While most potential deans and presidents will have difficulty finding even one good mentor, Gleazer's advice is nevertheless sound. Deans should be sensitive to their own roles as mentors, as well. If the dean needs a mentor to become president, it is just as likely that the division chair needs a mentor to become a dean. Having a mentor seems to be especially important to Hispanics, women, Blacks, and others who are currently making their way to the top of the administrative ladder. Deans from these groups should build upon their own experiences in order to fulfill the mentor's role more effectively and more often. A female dean reminds future deans not to "forget those other women coming behind you. They need the same help you got." Another dean offers a word of caution in relationship to your mentor: "Find a mentor who will support you, but do not sell your soul to that person." If you feel you have outgrown a mentor, find an advocate who has the influence to help you and who is willing to be your advocate.

*Establish a Peer Network.* Gleazer's advice that you get into the network is important. Indeed, his concept of mentoring, as outlined above, is more concerned with becoming a part of a professional network than it is with finding a single mentor, although mentoring in the classical sense is important to some individuals. The effective leader establishes and maintains a network of peers who can offer valuable advice, suggest professional opportunities, and serve as professional contacts and references. Community colleges are by definition somewhat provincial;

therefore, establishing a peer network requires a great deal of time and energy, but the pay-off for those who want to be a dean or president is worth the effort. (The ranking given peer networks by deans and presidents was a relative ranking and may reflect the thinking of members of these groups in terms of performing in their current role rather than in terms of someone who wants to move into a presidency or deanship.)

*Leadership Begins at Home.* Be visible on your own campus. Never miss an opportunity to address the faculty, but be sure you have something worth saying and are well prepared. Serve as the chair of important committees. As one dean suggests, volunteer for any number of assignments. Indeed, one of the nation's leading community college presidents places involvement in campus activities at the top of his list of advice for those who want to become a president: "More than anything else, people need to become visible and demonstrate that they are workers and creative and willing to do things. Volunteer to serve on committees, put in extra time, do the extra work without griping about it or asking if you are to be compensated. You will be quickly recognized, and you will be put into the channels to begin to move up." Certainly the same advice would apply to those who want to be deans of instruction. Take stands on important issues, especially those relating to the instructional program. Deans should address the governing board whenever possible, remembering to give plenty of credit to the president. Be friendly with the board, but not familiar. Develop a reputation for getting things done well and on time. Put your name on the reports and papers you produce. Serving as the author of a major campus study can quickly place a future dean in the spotlight, as many faculty members who have chaired an institutional self-study have discovered. Moreover, you never know when a document will be picked up and quoted both on and off campus, thereby increasing your visibility and reputation.

*Never, Ever, Base Your Career Upon What Someone Else Might Do.* While generalizations are dangerous when dealing with anything as complex as moving into the community college deanship or presidency (recall that one female dean had been waiting for several years for the deanship to become vacant at her institution before she successfully moved into the position), I believe it is safe to say that far too many chairs have missed their chance to become deans and too many deans have missed their opportunity to become presidents because they have waited around for the current dean or president to leave or retire. People have a nasty habit of not retiring when they say they will. In the case of deans, most effective ones have made about as many enemies on campus as friends; therefore, it often does not happen that the dean assumes the presidency on his or her own campus. The same situation, however, does not necessarily apply to those who aspire to the deanship, if for no other reason that their visibility (and chances to make enemies) has not been as high or as campus-wide.

*Become Involved in Community Activities.* Pick community activities that will enhance your chances of becoming a dean or a president and that will add to your effectiveness should you move into either (or ultimately both) positions. As cold-hearted as it may sound, the professional pay-off for working with the Chamber of Commerce is probably greater than it is for working with the Little Leagues.

*Be Willing to Move.* The majority of deanships and presidential vacancies are often somewhere else. The person who wants a deanship or a presidency must be willing to move to a new campus, a new town, a new state. To be "place-bound" often equates to being "career-bound." A veteran dean advises future deans to "be willing to move! Each step in my career path has meant a move to a new community." One successful president who is in his second presidency offers the following advice regarding moving: "If you are not restricted to a certain area of the country, then pick an area where you think there will be growth and go there." Women who are married must be especially sensitive to being stuck in a place where they have little or no chance of advancing in their careers.

*Be Willing to Move to the Hinterlands.* Most potential deans and presidents have their Camelot college in mind. They would like to have their first top leadership position in a place where the quality of life is excellent, the cost of living reasonable, the college high quality, and so on. Rarely is the ideal obtained in the first deanship or presidency. A national community college leader offers the following advice: "I think positioning would be the biggest piece of advice I would offer. Position yourself so that you're always in the right place at the right time. I advise some people to take a job though they know they will not stay there for a long time; just position yourself."

A word of caution is in order, however. Do not take a position just for the sake of becoming a dean or a president. The "fit" should be right for you and the college, and the position, while perhaps not the ultimate one, should be professionally rewarding. Take a position in the hinterlands, do outstanding work, and make plans to move to Camelot. Incidentally, you will probably find that you like that college off the beaten track much better than you think you will, and you will likely stay there much longer than you had expected to stay (a strong argument for establishing and maintaining a network of peers), so begin at once to make the best of the position, regardless of location.

Finally, a piece of advise from a dean that may well deserve to stand alone: "Retain tenure and the right to return to the faculty."

## APPLYING FOR THE POSITION: THE FIRST OFFICIAL ACT

William H. Meardy, former director of the Association of Community College Trustees (ACCT), offers sound advice to presidential applicants; his advice applies equally as well for aspirants to the deanship. The following appeared in his editorial, "A Shot in the Foot: Advice for Presidential Applicants."

> An all too common mistake, made by all too many applicants, is that they either do not know how to, or will not follow directions, as given in the advertisement. In nearly every ACCT-sponsored presidential search advertisement, there appears, IN BOLD PRINT, the following (or words to that effect): 'Applicants should state in writing how they meet the following criteria. COMPLIANCE WILL ENHANCE CONSIDERATION.' This directive does not say, 'A response to the following criteria must be found in the candidate's resume.' It has become apparent to me that many candidates read our request as, 'If it is found in my resume, I don't need to respond.' That is not at all what the advertisement requests. Thus the candidate following this line of reasoning has already shot himself or herself in the foot. Other candidates put themselves at an immediate disadvantage with typographical errors, poor grammar, or by leaving some criteria without a response. The lack of a response will necessarily raise questions in the reader's mind. Remember that in most cases, the team of readers have never met you and do not know of your abilities. Therefore, your application must be letter perfect. Almost perfect will not carry the day for you. What board wants to employ a president who cannot follow directions or is sloppy in production? [Nor does any president want to employ a dean of instruction who cannot follow directions or is sloppy in production.] The competition is just too keen to take a chance on an applicant who has already exposed potential flaws (quoted in Vaughan, 1989b, pp. 128–129).

• • •

### What to Do

While keeping Meardy's excellent advice in mind, the following suggestions, some of which seem elementary but all of which are drawn from actual situations, may further enhance one's chances of being seriously considered for the deanship or the presidency.

*Have Your Letter and Application Typed.* It is amazing that someone who is seeking a position with an annual salary of $50,000 to $80,000 will not spend the few dollars it costs to have an application typed, for it is well worth the cost. It becomes even more amazing when one knows that the person making an application (especially if he or she is a dean) has rejected any number of applicants because of a sloppy application. Make a copy of the application and complete it before completing the original. By completing the copy, you can make sure that the information will fit into the spaces provided. One consultant states: "As simple as it may seem, not developing a 'professional-looking' application packet is a common error made by individuals applying for the presidency." While there is no consensus on the topic, you probably should not use your current institution's stationery when applying for a position outside of your own institution.

*Be Careful About Listing Professional Organizations.* List only those organizations to which you currently belong. Some member of the dean's selection committee or a member of the governing board's presidential screening committee is likely to belong to the organization you list and to which you have not paid your dues for years. The question you might get about the organization may embarrass you, at the least, and lose you the position at the worst. Do not list institutional memberships under your own professional membership. For example, membership in the AACJC, an organization in which most memberships are institutional, often shows up on resumes. There are some legitimate crossovers, however. The affiliate councils of the AACJC, NACUBO, and its regional branches and other organizations often offer individual memberships as a part of the institutional membership package.

*Sign Your Application and Covering Letter.* As elementary as it may seem, individuals sometimes forget to sign their letters of application (one of the inherent dangers of having someone else type the application), an error that in many cases invalidates the application and, in any event, shows a lack of attention to important details. To ensure that you have signed your application, prepare a check-list which includes, among other things, checking for your signature. Also, have someone else review the application for you.

*Write the Letter of Application for the Position for Which You Are Applying.* A quote from a consultant who has reviewed literally thousands of applications serves to make this point. "I have seen the same letter used to apply for the presidency of a small rural college with an enrollment of under 1,000 and to an urban community college with thousands and thousands of students and very complex dynamics." Another consultant sees a common error as "sending the same application (no matter how good) to every opening across the country. Develop 'original' applications for each situation." No matter how good the application package is, consultants soon recognize the same package and an "Oh no, not again" syndrome develops. For example, I have seen *exactly* the same package go to four different colleges in one state.

*Pay Careful Attention to the "Profile" Developed for the Position.* The criteria published in the position announcement should be read carefully and each point should be addressed specifically. As pointed out rather dramatically in the Meardy quote, today more and more governing boards and college search committees are developing a rather specific list of characteristics and qualifications they are seeking in deans and presidents. Some candidates fail to understand that governing boards and consultants put a lot of effort and money into developing the profile for the position and consider it to be very important. To quote a consultant: "It is almost as if some applicants can't read, even though they may possess a Ph.D. degree. The other conclusion would be that there is no concern for the request for information, which is equally as damaging."

*Have Someone Check Your Grammar.* Spelling errors should not appear on applications for employment in any segment of society; they are especially damaging when found on applications for the deanship and presidency. While some search committees tend to be generous with spelling errors, often passing them off as typographical errors, the same is not true of grammatical mistakes, such as subject-verb agreement. Although faulty subject-verb agreements and other mistakes are less common than "typos," they are more deadly when made. Although community college deans and presidents may not be scholars in the traditional sense of the term, they should be able to write a letter of application that is free of grammatical errors.

*Follow the Directions Given on the Application.* If the application asks for your academic degrees and requests that you list the last one first, then list the last one first, even if your resume follows a different format. Be clear. A consultant notes that "candidates make it difficult to find dates, e.g., degrees received, where and when; places worked, etc. You have to hunt for these 'nuggets' in a very disorganized resume."

*Meet the Deadline for the Application.* You may think, "So I missed the deadline, so what." Unfortunately, you have sent a signal that the position was not that important to you anyway. This message can be especially deadly to an internal candidate who seeks to move into the deanship or presidency on his or her own campus. Late applications also show an insensitivity to the search process, which costs thousands of dollars and consumes many hours of time for a number of individuals. Moreover, although your application is late, it may still be seen by the search committee or a consultant who will remember seeing it, and if it shows up in a different applicant pool at a later date, the consultant will have a negative image associated with your application. If you cannot make the deadline for a particular position, forget it, for your application will not be considered. Instead of wasting everyone's time, wait until a position comes along in which you are interested enough to meet the application deadline.

*Fill in All Spaces on the Application.* A "not applicable" might be appropriate, but put something in the blank. If your current salary is asked for, give the salary you currently earn and not what you project to earn next year, even if you are only one month away from a new salary. Do not fudge here, for you are likely to get caught. Even if you are not caught at the moment, you have acted unprofessionally; moreover, you have falsified your application, and no one wants to employ someone who lies on an application.

*Do Not Leave Gaps in Your Employment History Without a Proper Explanation.* If you spent two years in military service, list the two years; if you took three years off to concentrate on raising a family, list the time off and explain what you were doing. If you returned to graduate school, let the search committee know this. Search committees should not be expected to guess what someone did for a couple of years. Indeed, most search committees will not guess; they will simply eliminate an application that is incomplete or confusing. Internal candidates cannot assume the search committee knows one's qualifications and employment history; therefore, internal candidates must have a complete and current resume for the committee's review. Most resumes contain a number of surprises, even for the colleague down the hall.

*Either List Your Current Supervisor as a Reference or Explain Why You Do Not.* The fact that you may view the supervisor as incompetent is not a good-enough reason for not listing the person. Most careful search processes demand that a check be made with one's current supervisor. The reference check of the supervisor may be delayed, upon request, pending your making the "final cut" for the interviews. If you desire that the reference check of the immediate supervisor be delayed, make the request at the time you submit your application, but be prepared to have the immediate supervisor contacted if you become a serious candidate for a position.

*Do Not Try to Incorporate Your Life's History into Your Letter of Application.* If you wish to include a statement of your educational philosophy, do so in an attachment or as specified in the directions outlined in the position announcement. Remember that literally everyone has a philosophy of education and that most people will likely disagree with parts of yours, therefore likely opening up the wrong debate in the interview. If you include a statement on your educational philosophy, be brief, be general, and be careful. The statement should be well-written and grammatically correct. Avoid what one consultant calls "high-school-level essays about your philosophy of education." Another consultant warns against including a photograph taken for another purpose. For example, the picture taken for the college yearbook, no matter how attractive, just might not be appropriate for your application some 20 years later. The best advice is not to include a photo unless one is requested.

*Do Not Include Irrelevant Material with the Application.* Everyone I have ever talked with on the subject of presidential selection, including faculty, administrators, and board members, resents getting a lot of attachments that are only indirectly (if at all) related to the position applied for. As one consultant notes: "Candidates inundate you with extraneous material, i.e., copies of articles they have written, their district's long-range plan," and other material that has little to do with the position at hand.

*Give an Indication That You Understand the Nature of the Position for Which You Are Applying.* Governing boards and faculty want presidential applicants who not only understand the deanship or presidency at the particular college to which they are applying, but who also understand it as a professional position with universal characteristics. Talk with friends and colleagues who understand the position. Ask your mentor for advice.

*Do Not List People as References Who Hardly Know You.* Do not make amateurish attempts to use political influence. If you list someone as a reference, make sure the person knows your ability to perform in the position for which you have applied and be reasonably sure your reference will support your candidacy. Do not list more references than requested. (I recall one unsuccessful applicant who listed 21 references.) If no set number of references is requested, you should probably list three and no more than five.

*Watch the Word Processor.* Make sure you include only the name of the college to which you are applying, eliminating all references to the last college to which you sent your letter of application. This advice may sound amusing; however, cases exist where letters of application name one college in one paragraph and another college in another place in the same letter. If you use a form letter, and remember that one of the consultants cited above warns against this practice, make sure you remove the name of the previous college to which you applied.

*Do Not Send Too Many "25-Centers."* The practice of sending out multiple applications by rationalizing that they only cost the 25 cents spent on a postage stamp is a poor one. That is, be careful about flooding the market with applications for positions in which you have little interest. As is true in being late with your application, word gets around when you casually apply for practically every position that comes along. On the other hand, do not be bashful about applying for positions if you feel they are professionally correct for you. Some deans have been interviewed as many as seven, eight, nine, or 10 times before obtaining a presidency, and certainly many division chairs and others fail to be selected as a dean the first time they apply.

*Send the Application to the Person Who is Supposed to Receive It.* For example, if it is to go to the personnel director or the chair of the search committee, send it to the correct person, not to the chairperson of the governing board, even if the chair lives next door. This advice is especially important if you are an internal candidate, even though you may know where the application will ultimately go. Do not send the application to the current president of the college unless you are directed to do so, no matter how well you may know the individual. You are almost guaranteed to turn off the search committee and others by bypassing the established process.

## THE INTERVIEW PROCESS: AVOID THE COMMON MISTAKES

While getting the interview is noteworthy, it hardly guarantees that you will be offered the position. The way you conduct yourself before, during, and after the interview is as important, if not more so, as how you complete your application materials. The following suggestions should assist you in planning for the interview process.

*Be On Time for the Interview.* This is so basic that nothing else needs to be said about it here, yet I know of one applicant for a dean's position who lost the position because she was late for her most important appointment.

*Prepare for the Interview.* You should be familiar with the institution to which you apply. Preparing for the interview includes knowing about the college's enrollment, programs of study, composition of faculty and staff, budget, service region, results of recent self-studies, assets, liabilities, and other relevant information. One consultant advises presidential candidates to "study the auditor's report and don't hesitate to ask penetrating questions" (Weintraub, 1987, p. 5). Write the institution for information on the college; write the Chamber of Commerce or similar organizations for information on the area. A good approach is to subscribe to the local newspapers as far in advance of the interview as possible. You should also subscribe to weekly or semiweekly newspapers, if you are applying to a college located in a rural area, and to newspapers that cater primarily to minorities, if such papers exist in the college's service region. Know the names and positions of the trustees in advance, and if possible know the constituency each trustee represents. For example, if you have a Black trustee from a Black section of the city, you should not be shocked when you are asked a question related to how the community college should serve Blacks. (It may be doing quite well; you should know this, however.) Know the local, state, and national political leaders and their relationship to the college.

*Arrive in Town a Day or Two Early.* For out-of-town interviews, the entire family should accompany you (to the city—*not* the interview) if you are married and if possible. At the very least, your spouse should accompany you. Checkout the cost of housing (you should have obtained information on housing from the Chamber of Commerce; if not, obtain it from a real estate agent), the reputation of the public schools, and the types and availability of churches, as well as service, social, recreational and cultural organizations. Get a general feeling for the community. You should also take a "straw poll" of the citizens (hotel clerks, waitresses, cabdrivers, real estate agents, school principals, and the "person on the street") to see how the college is viewed by members of the community.

*Dress for the Occasion.* Candidates should dress in a style that is suitable for the area in which the college is located. A suit with a western flair might be a big hit in west Texas but will likely lose you the position in Boston or Key West. Shoes are important: boots are out. I recall an incident some years ago when a male applicant for a public school superintendency (he was a superintendent at the time he applied but wanted to move to a larger system) was told by the board members that he lost a position in their city because he wore dress boots to the interview. A male dean of instruction was eliminated from consideration for a presidency because he wore Western boots to the interview. Many governing boards have a cocktail party and dinner for presidential applicants the night before or after the interview. Male candidates should wear a dark suit, a white non-button-down shirt, and an appropriate necktie. Female candidates should dress accordingly, keeping accessories unobtrusive and to a minimum. The spouse of the candidate also should dress appropriately. Internal candidates for the deanship or presidency should not ignore these suggestions; rather, if anything, the internal candidate should be extra sensitive to presenting an image in concert with the deanship or presidency, taking nothing for granted.

*Wait to Be Asked.* Do not assume anything, including taking a seat, until you are invited to do so. Sit up straight; talk plainly and at a level that is appropriate for the room and the situation. Exercise common sense, including good manners.

*To Drink or Not to Drink is Not the Question: The Question is What to Drink and How Much.* The question of whether to drink alcohol at a board reception is a touchy one. Certainly, if a board has a cocktail party and if the candidate uses alcohol (*never* have a drink containing alcohol if its use is against your beliefs), one drink will do no harm and may help the mood of the evening. On the other hand, neither the candidate nor the spouse should *ever* have enough alcohol during the evening to "feel it." The board may well be in a partying mood; however, neither the candidate nor the spouse of the candidate can afford to be sucked into the party, no matter how much fun the board chair is having. The board will not still love you tomorrow unless your actions are beyond reproach the night before. On the other hand, the candidate and spouse should drink something (not necessarily alcohol) at the cocktail party. Nothing is more disquieting at a cocktail party than to have the guests of honor stand around, arms folded, while others enjoy their drinks. Drinking, or at least holding a glass of mineral water with a twist of lime, occupies the hands and permits the candidate to be a part of the group rather than a bystander.

*Do Not Criticize Your Current Dean or President.* Word gets around if you criticize those with whom you work; moreover, criticisms of the person for whom you work may be taken as a sign of disloyalty and even incompetency on your part. If something is wrong at your current college, you should be playing a major role in correcting the problem rather than criticizing the current dean or president.

*Do Not Give the Impression That You Are Trying to Leave a Place.* Rather than giving the impression that you want to leave your current position, convey the message that you are interested in furthering your professional career by moving into a position with more responsibility and perhaps more rewards. State why you are seeking the position. Most colleges do not want a person as a dean or president who is running away from his or her current position and see the new position as an escape route.

*Be Yourself During the Interview, But Do Not Work Too Hard at Being Just "One of the Guys or One of the Gals."* Relax some, but not too much. Do not take off your coat or loosen your tie if you are a male, or otherwise make yourself comfortable, no matter what invitation is extended to you by those doing the interviewing. Do not smoke unless it is a very, very informal situation and unless several others present are smoking.

*Be a Good Listener.* Respond to the questions you are asked and shut up. For example, if you are asked how you would handle a potential legal problem, give a brief answer; do not respond with briefs on all of the cases dealing with the question at hand. As one well-known former chancellor and present consultant for presidential searches observes: "Too many candidates work at being profound, too profound."

*Be Honest.* Do not equivocate. If you are caught in a lie, you have probably lost the position. For example, when asked how many people you currently supervise, do not list a number equal to the total faculty. (Moreover, many faculty committees resent the implication that they are being "supervised" by anyone and certainly do not want a dean or president coming into a position to supervise them.) If you do not know something, say so and move on. On the other hand, you cannot afford too many "I don't knows," a situation that is unlikely to exist if you prepare for the interview.

*Never Talk Down to An Interviewer.* This advice is especially true when you talk with your colleagues within an institution if you are an internal candidate for the deanship; of course, presidential candidates should never talk down to the governing board. Remember, you have the primary responsibility to adapt to the interviewer and not vice versa. On the other hand, be subtle in controlling how the interview progresses. Do not play up to one particular committee member, even if the person is a friend. You may win one vote but lose a dozen. Ideally, the interview should be a conversation with the focus of the conversation on you, the candidate.

*If You Are Married, Discuss the Role of the Spouse.* This advice applies more to presidential applicants than to those applying for the deanship; nevertheless, as illustrated earlier, some search committee members have some rather strange concepts about the role of the spouse, especially if you are a female candidate for the deanship. If you are selected president, does the governing board expect the spouse to entertain at home? If so, are funds and support services available? Is the spouse a professional person in his or her own right? If so, let the board know this during the interview, for some boards still think that when they employ a married president (especially if the president is male), they are getting "two for the price of one," although this belief is not as common today as it was in the past. Most dean's searches give scant attention to the role of the spouse. On the other hand, ideally, the spouse of presidential applicants should be interviewed by the board if the board has any expectations of the spouse or if the spouse has any expectations of the board.

*Ask Questions About Salary, Fringe Benefits, Expectations, Anything and Everything, During the Interview.* If you wait until after you sign a contract to discuss salary and similar issues, it is too late. Discuss your "compromise line," and you must have one. For example, applicants for the deanship should let the president and members of the college community know the practices they will follow in employing college personnel and that they will not compromise on personnel practices, no matter who recommends whom for employment at the college. Presidential applicants should be just as careful in informing the governing board of their views on employment and other relevant matters. However, do not be argumentative during the interview. Make your point as clearly as possible, but do not go to war with the person asking the question, especially over trivial points that have little or nothing to do with how you would function as dean or president. Stated another way, the interview is neither the time nor place to have a showdown with the chair of the faculty senate, the board chair, or anyone else for that matter. If the salary is unacceptable, say so and tell why. But do not alienate members of the college community or the board, for even if your salary demands are met, you may well be off to a bad start in your new position.

When considering negotiations during the interview, keep in mind the advice offered by Ruth G. Weintraub, senior vice president of the Academy for Educational Development and director of its Executive Search Division. She cautions: "Don't do any negotiating until you have a clear sense that you are the preferred candidate" (Weintraub, 1987, p. 5). That is, do not make too many demands for salary, fringe benefits, and other items that might be negotiable until you have a good idea that you are the one the board is interested in negotiating with.

*Be Careful About How You Use Personal Pronouns.* You want to give yourself credit for what you have done, but do not appear to take total credit. No one does it alone. For example, I recommend that you never refer to "*my* faculty" or "*my* administrators." It is just as easy and certainly more realistic to talk about our faculty or the college's faculty.

*Make Sure You Are Prepared to Take the Position if It is Offered, Assuming It is Professionally Right for You and the Institution.* This suggestion does not imply that every position you apply for is the right one for you and should be accepted if offered. But if you reject the position, do it for professional reasons, not because you cannot take the children out of school, sell your house, afford the current mortgage rate, or leave your aging parents. You are already aware that these situations represent potential problems; deal with them before you apply for a position. Again, word gets around from college to college and from consultants, so if you drop out of one deanship or presidential race because of existing personal reasons, you may be hurt when you apply for future positions. If you are not willing to move unless your spouse can find a suitable position in the new community, state this in your application and during the interview, not after the position is offered.

## When All Else Is Considered

Following the above suggestions will in no way guarantee that you will obtain a community college deanship or presidency; however, these suggestions may well help you avoid "shooting yourself in the foot," to use William Meardy's descriptive phrase. By avoiding needless errors, using good judgment in preparing for positions, working hard, having the right experience and degrees, being in the right place at the right time, and having a bit of luck, you can likely obtain the community college deanship or presidency, assuming of course that the interview indicates that the "chemistry," or "fit," is right between you, the search committee, the college president in the case of the deanship, the college board in case of the presidency, the college community, and the community at large.

## WHAT TO EXPECT UPON BECOMING PRESIDENT

This volume is devoted, in part, to describing what one can expect upon becoming a dean of instruction. Future deans are presented with a profile of the current deans, as well as obstacles the aspiring dean may face on the pathway to the deanship.

What can current deans expect (other than the unexpected) upon assuming the presidency? A well-known former chancellor of a major community college system sets the stage for this discussion with the following advice. "As president, expect to work a hell of a lot. Do not go into the presidency because it is going to be prestigious, because you'll have some cards that say president, because you will have a big desk and people will call you president. Go in for the right reasons, and I think the right reasons are commitment, and the belief that your presence is going to make a difference. And you are going to make a difference by working hard, by giving whatever talents you have, and by causing good things to happen. If you plan to go in for other reasons, you shouldn't go in. And if you do you should be kicked out."

A president admonishes those deans who would be president "to realize that the president's role has changed dramatically from one of an academic role to one of almost a manager of the institution." This advice is especially relevant for those deans of instruction who will be tempted to continue to "play dean" once they become president. Whereas the dean of instruction's position is by definition concerned almost totally with faculty concerns and the instructional program, the president must be concerned with students, staff, the other deans (some of whom may have been viewed as "the enemy" if one assumes the presidency on the campus where he or she is dean), and literally every member of the college community.

Expect to devote what may appear to be an inordinate amount of time and energy to the political process, especially to those political entities that provide funding for the college. Most deans and others who move into the presidency have almost no experience in the political realm; however, if they are to be effective presidents, they must master the process quickly and often with little help, especially in the smaller community colleges.

Another area in which the new president can expect to find frustrations and rewards is in working with the governing board. As is the case with the political process, most individuals new to the presidency have little concept of the time, energy, and skillful planning that goes into the "care and feeding" of the board.

Although the new president can expect to have many of the latest management tools available, this in no way replaces the necessity of dealing with people. Indeed, as society has become more impersonal—as more and more members of the academic community spend more and more time hunched over computers—the presidency requires a better use of interpersonal skills than ever before in the history of the community college. New presidents, as has always been true, must realize that people still need people and act accordingly. Intuition, not computer printouts, may be the most valuable tool a president possesses. At any rate, the successful president must relate well with members of the college community and with external constituents.

The president can expect the governance process to be more complicated at the presidential level than at other levels within the college. If the new presidency is to be on a unionized campus and the candidate has never worked in a unionized situation, the governance process will take on an important new dimension. The dean of instruction who has spent a career promoting the academic point of view in the governance of the institution must, as president, have a broader view, a view that may conflict with some views held as a dean.

Upon assuming the presidency, one can expect to spend more time not only with political leaders, but with other external constituents as well. The external role of the president is very demanding, and there never seems to be enough time to spend with local business and labor leaders, the Chamber of Commerce, or any number of various clubs and organizations that expect the president to join them, work with them, speak to them, or otherwise support them.

Expect to feel pressure to raise funds from private sources. The college foundation continues to assume importance on many campuses, and the president is expected to provide leadership for the foundation, including calling on potential donors.

The president can expect to deal with pressure groups that, prior to assuming the presidency, he or she did not even know existed. The pressure groups will make demands that are impossible to meet but nevertheless cannot be ignored.

The new president can expect to lose some friends and can expect some feelings of alienation to occur from all segments of the college community. If one assumes the presidency on one's own campus, even old and dear friends on the faculty and staff often become distant. The phrase "lonely at the top" takes on new meaning once the "top" is reached. On the other hand, the president can expect to make new friends, many of whom will be presidential colleagues.

The new president needs to understand the traditions of the institution and work to preserve them. Just as important, perhaps, is the need to establish new traditions, for most community colleges are short on tradition. The traditions must enhance the institution's standing in the academic community and the community at large and must not be viewed as idiosyncrasies of the president.

The president can expect to be called upon to exercise good judgment, to communicate effectively in writing and speaking, to maintain institutional and personal integrity, to act and think courageously, and to exercise other accepted characteristics of good leadership that have been around for thousands of years.

Finally, as a community college president, you can expect to occupy the most exciting position on campus and perhaps in all of higher education. As one president describes the presidency, "When it is good, it is very, very good."

# 9

# Conclusions and
# Recommendations

■

The book began with the question: "What is a dean of instruction?" It was never anticipated that answering the question would be easy, and it was not. Indeed, much of what is discussed here is subjective, for no attempt was made to produce a scientific study with a statistical base. Moreover, anytime a white man talks subjectively about women, Blacks, and Hispanics, there are bound to be gaps in the conversation. Nevertheless, the foregoing chapters provide some answers to the question, while recognizing that many questions remain to be answered regarding the dean of instruction's position.

As anyone who has ever attempted to write about any aspect of the community college realizes, it is difficult and somewhat dangerous to generalize about anything as complex as the nation's community colleges. The complexities multiply when one generalizes about the dean of instruction's position, for in the final analysis you are not talking about some generic position, but rather about more than 1,100 individuals who serve as their institution's chief academic officers and who see their role from a perspective unavailable to anyone else. But generalize we must.

Generalizations also bring some disagreements from almost everyone, which is not a bad thing for institutions devoted to the search for truth and knowledge. Generalizations aside, I believe most of the chief academic officers in the nation's community colleges will recognize themselves and their colleagues throughout much of the preceding discussion.

The following conclusions and recommendations provide an ending for the current study. If the book is successful, they will serve, in part, as the starting point for others interested in studying the dean of instruction's position. If this happens, the book will have been an overwhelming success.

## CONCLUSION 1 AND RECOMMENDATIONS

### Conclusion

The overwhelming conclusion reached in this study is that current deans of instruction are almost mirror images of current presidents, with the exception that more of the current deans are women than are current presidents. Even in the case of women, the backgrounds of current deans is quite similar to the backgrounds of presidents. Further, with the exception of more women now waiting in the presidential pipeline, future presidents will resemble current presidents in almost every aspect. There are negative and positive aspects to the current deans being mirror images of current presidents. From a positive point of view, community colleges are now mature enough to produce their own leaders, without turning to four-year institutions or the public schools for these leaders, as was often the case in the 1960s, thereby ensuring continuity in leadership. On the negative side, if the profile of the community college's top leaders does not change and if the pathway to the presidency remains the traditional one, the pool of minority leaders in the presidential pipeline is so small that community college presidents of the future will be largely white, with white men continuing to occupy an inordinate number of the presidencies. (In *Leadership in Transition* [Vaughan, 1989b], I concluded that there would likely be more minority community college presidents in the future. Based on this study of the deans, I no longer feel that this will be the case.) This situation will exist at a time when more and more of the students enrolled in the community colleges are racial and ethnic minorities, especially Blacks and Hispanics.

### Recommendations

*Recommendation.* The community college should continue and increase its efforts to move women into the chief academic officer's position, thereby assuring that in the future the supply of potential women presidents is adequate to meet the needs of the future.

*Recommendation.* Female deans should view the presidency as within their reach and make it a career goal, assuming that they desire the position.

*Recommendation.* More minority faculty members must be recruited, and more minority faculty members must be encouraged to enter community college administration.

*Recommendation.* Minority deans must be encouraged to become community college presidents, and vacant deanships should be filled with a minority, when possible. Affirmative action policies should be strictly adhered to both in spirit as well as legally.

*Recommendation.* Current presidents and deans of instruction must diminish the image and the reality of the all-white, all-male, "old boys' club" (possibly a remnant from their blue-collar past) and welcome minorities and women into every professional activity expected of top community college leaders. Minority professionals must be made to feel welcome at predominantly white institutions as well as at those with large minority populations.

*Recommendation.* If minorities are to make any major inroads into the top two ranks of community college administration, they must have role models and mentors. Until the time that enough minorities enter the top ranks of community college leadership, white presidents and deans must put forth a special effort to serve as mentors for minorities.

*Recommendation.* Women should continue and expand their efforts at providing professional networks for other women. Included in the network of professional contacts should be women who are willing to serve as mentors to other women. Women on individual campuses should also make every effort possible to serve as mentors for other women.

*Recommendation.* Minorities need to strengthen their peer networks and make it possible for more minorities to take advantage of the networks.

*Recommendation.* Minority groups other than Blacks and Hispanics should establish affiliate councils of the AACJC. For example, Asian community college professionals would be one group that could profit from its own council. The same might be true for community college professionals who are Americans Indians.

*Recommendation.* The AACJC must begin to collect data on the race, ethnicity, and sex of community college leaders. This emphasis on data collection on minorities should be apart of AACJC's new Minority Education Initiative.

## CONCLUSION 2 AND RECOMMENDATIONS

### Conclusion

The statement is made early in the volume that the dean of instruction has the responsibility to ensure that the college does not stray from its central mission of teaching and learning. This statement raises a number of questions, many of which go to the very heart of the community college's mission. For example, is the dean of instruction to be held responsible for the teaching and learning that takes place in community services divisions, many of which operate independently of the regular instructional program? Is the dean of instruction to be responsible for the many different types of programs community colleges conduct with business and industry? The conclusion reached after completing this study is that the dean of instruction should be responsible for all teaching and learning that takes place through the college's instructional program for which college credit or continuing education units are awarded, regardless of the nature or location of the instruction.

### Recommendations

*Recommendation.* As the institution's chief academic officer, the dean of instruction should have the responsibility for all academic programs and courses, including community services, if the community services division awards credit for its instruction.

*Recommendation.* In those situations where the college has a dean of community services who is equal on the organizational chart to the dean of instruction, the organization should be changed in a way that causes the person in charge of community services to report to the chief academic officer, assuming the community services division offers courses for credit.

## CONCLUSION 3 AND RECOMMENDATIONS

### Conclusion

The majority of the deans of instruction, as is true with the majority of the community college presidents, come from blue collar backgrounds. The conclusion is that the blue-collar background of deans of instruction make them more empathic with the backgrounds of the majority of the community college's students. Moreover, the blue-collar background makes the deans more willing to accept and promote the community college's comprehensive mission, especially technical education. Finally, and this conclusion is tentative, part of the defensiveness community college leaders exhibit when criticized is due to their blue-collar background, resulting in the community college suffering from an image of anti-intellectualism.

## Recommendations

*Recommendation.* Community college leaders should communicate to the public that for many of the students served by the community college, technical education is a vehicle for social advancement and is not, as some critics claim, a means of repressing student ambitions or of cooling out students.

*Recommendation.* Community college leaders should react to criticism of the community college unemotionally, basing their responses to the critics on research. Moreover, when criticized, community college leaders should use the opportunity to enlighten the public to the mission of the community college and to how the mission is be fulfilled.

# CONCLUSION 4 AND RECOMMENDATIONS

## Conclusion

The deans of instruction are concerned about and interested in promoting scholarship in the community college. They feel, however, that due to the workload of faculty and administrators, scholarship must occupy a low priority among community college professionals.

## Recommendations

*Recommendation.* Deans must resist the temptation to become bogged down in bureaucratic chores that leave little or no time for thinking and engaging in scholarship. Deans need to realize that a point of diminishing returns occurs well before the day-to-day tasks are completed; therefore, by stepping back from the daily tasks, efficiency may well be increased in all aspects of the dean's position.

*Recommendation.* Deans should make faculty and other administrators aware of the dean's interest in and commitment to scholarship and establish mechanisms for recognizing and rewarding scholarship.

*Recommendation.* Deans should devote some time each day to keeping up with the scholarly work being done in higher education, with special emphasis on the community college, and commit themselves to producing scholarly work that is in concert with the definition of scholarship presented in Chapter 7 of this volume, or a definition that is accepted by the college community.

*Recommendation.* Deans should encourage presidents to join them in promoting scholarship on the individual campus and nationally.

## CONCLUSION 5 AND RECOMMENDATIONS

### Conclusion

Deans of instruction occupy that middle ground between the president and the faculty and must constantly and effectively represent the views of the college's top administration and faculty. Yet, as noted, only approximately 33 percent of the deans view the president as their chief confidant, and none of the deans view their primary relationship with the faculty as that of colleague. The dean's position, then, is somewhat isolated in spite of being at the crossroads of much of what happens at the college.

### Recommendations

*Recommendation.* Presidents should be sensitive to the dean's role as the institution's chief advocate of teaching and learning and should open the door to their office to the dean at all times, providing support for the dean, and serving as the dean's confidant at all times. Presidents should realize that the dean's position, as is true with the president's position, is a lonely one.

*Recommendation.* The faculty should be sensitive to the dean's position and explore avenues for including the dean in discussions that go beyond the normal duties of the dean's office. Mutual ground might be a discussion of the role of scholarship among community college professionals.

*Recommendation.* Deans should take advantage of their place in the middle and use it to enhance communications between the faculty and the president by illustrating to both that mutual respect and mutual interests must be a part of the culture of the effective community college. Deans can enhance their own image and effectiveness by bringing issues that are of concern to all community college professionals to the forefront and seeing that the issues are discussed in a professional manner.

## A FINAL WORD

It seems only fitting that the deans of instruction have the final word in a book devoted to understanding their roles. A number of deans were asked during the interview where they feel presidents fail in their relationship with chief academic officers and what advice they, the deans, would offer community college presidents in order that presidents can utilize deans more effectively.

## Deans on Presidents

The president-dean of instruction relationship is second only to the president-board relationship in charting the course of the individual community college. Based upon my conversations with deans and presidents, most deans and presidents realize this and work well together. Deans do, however, have some concerns and advice for presidents. They can be summarized as follows:

- Deans want presidents to listen and to be open with them, sharing all information that will help them do their job more effectively.

- Deans want to share in the glory and the accomplishments of the institution.

- Deans especially want presidents who are former chief academic officers to "let go" and not continue to "play dean" once they become president.

- Deans want clear direction from the president, including knowing what the president's vision for the institution's future is and what is expected of the dean in accomplishing that vision.

- Deans want the president to support their decisions, for as one dean notes, "When I take the risk, when I go out and put it on the line, I want to know that the rug's not going to be pulled from under me. And if it ever once is, you can guarantee the dean's not going to take any more risks."

- Deans want to be given direction and then left alone to perform their work without undue interference from the president.

- Deans want to know how the president views their performance, with the president providing deans with constant "feedback."

- Deans want to be able to disagree with the president, when appropriate, and to propose alternate courses of action to those proposed by the president, assuming that a number of the alternatives will be accepted.

- Deans want the freedom and encouragement to grow and develop to their full potential, including gaining more knowledge and assuming increasing responsibility in areas that extend beyond the instructional program.

- Deans want the president to serve as their mentor, including serving as their advocate should the dean seek a presidency or any other position.

- Deans who want to become a president want presidents to teach them more about the external aspects of the presidency, including legislative work, working with the board, and fund raising.

- Deans want to be accepted and acknowledged by the president as important members of the college's leadership team, a team devoted to enhancing the educational process for all who teach and learn at the nation's community colleges.

- Finally, deans want presidents to slow down, to develop patience, to realize that community colleges are not built in a day.

In order to get a better understanding of what deans want, the following quotes let the deans speak for themselves.

From a dean who traveled the traditional pathway to the presidency, maintaining close ties with the faculty:

*I expect the president to be open. I expect him to share information about either state or local funding openly with the deans. I expect him to provide a very clear definition of where he believes the institution ought to be going, the kinds of policies and programs he would like to see instituted, and provide opportunities for us to discuss those ideas openly, and for me to be able to pose alternatives if I believe there ought to be some, to object when I feel they're inappropriate, and then, ultimately, to allow me to carry out the day-to-day instructional operations without interference.*

• • •

From a female dean: "You need to turn that off [the tape recorder] and let me think about it.... O.K. If presidents come from the role of deans, they think that the president should be the chief instructional leader on campus, and I think that's a mistake. Sometimes I think it's a little hard for them to turn loose of the things that they did as dean and to let the dean go out and do the things he or she needs to do."

Another dean thinks that presidents fail because they never share enough information with the dean and because they do not make their expectations clear. Another dean believes that presidents:

*Take too much ownership in the organization, personally, where they become the father of the organization, and they take on the authoritative role of that father or mother of the organization. I think a failure is not allowing individuals to take risks, to make decisions. I think it's a very critical role of presidents to develop future leaders, for the whole community college movement is based upon evolution, and evolution means that at every generation there's a new set of leaders that needs to be developed. I think the president needs to take on that role and responsibility, and I think in some cases, because of discomfort, uncomfortableness with a strong person at their right hand or left hand, that they in effect have kept that person under their thumb, not allowing them to grow, not allowing them to mature, not allowing them to experiment, not allowing them to take some of the glory or success.*

• • •

Another dean believes that many presidents fail when they do not support the decisions of the dean and permit members of the college community to circumvent the organizational structure by going around the dean: "I think that if a president allows other groups to come around the vice president or dean and responds directly to them, that undermines the role of the dean or vice president. And I think you can fail that way."

## Advice from Deans to Presidents

Some advice from the deans of instruction serve to remind presidents that deans have their own opinions of how things should be done. From one dean comes the advice that presidents should support deans and let the deans "share some of the glory. I think they need to be mentors to the dean and to do what they can to develop a kind of close personal relationship." From another dean: "Well, make it a team. To really go after it in terms of the way you would go after winning a game, being a successful team. I think that if the president can lead by bringing along the other staff members, they will all work together to succeed." Similarly, from another dean:

*I think I would encourage presidents to take the academic deans strongly into a partnership when it comes to leadership of the institution, to find a very significant role, side-kick role, right alongside the president when it comes to laying out strategic plans for the college. In my own way of thinking, the academic dean is probably the most critical person aside from the president in developing an effective instructional program.*

• • •

Presidents are known for their impatience. One dean suggests that presidents "move too quickly. I think, as a vice president, the one thing I've learned is to slow down and to be more patient and [know] that there are many processes I could set in place. I could make them up in one night, but when you have to bring the others along and do it by committee, you learn to go slowly. The president has to understand that the process takes time also, and be patient." Similarly from a 15-year veteran dean:

*Sometimes [the president] does not understand how difficult it may be working with people who do not have those same priorities [as the president] or the same speed in mind. Faculty in particular. There has to be an understanding that there are the vested interest groups. There are people at the institution who have their little areas that need to be protected. The faculty, in particular, I'm talking about, have tremendous anxieties about change, and I think [presidents] have to understand that change sometimes cannot come as quickly as presidents would like. I think that not understanding this is a major failure of presidents.*

• • •

From a former dean who is now a president comes the following advice. He acknowledges that the president's role is in running the institution and dealing with external relationships, but he asks:

*What about the morale of the organization, the implementation of policy, or the implementation of specific goals, [all of which are] tied to the ability of the dean to provide leadership to the division chairs, and of division chairs to lead the faculty. It's a multi-tiered process, and I think presidents have to recognize that, have to cultivate growth and leadership, not only from the deans, but all the way down to the division chairs and to faculty, who could, in turn, take on the role of division chair.*

• • •

Finally, one dean advises presidents to look to the dean for leadership beyond the instructional program and realize that "the sharing of information and discussions that ought to go on within the president's office need to be open, clear, and objective, and that disagreements can occur. But ultimately, when everyone walks out of that office, there is some clear understanding of what needs to be done."

## The Future

Based upon this quick look at the dean of instruction's position, it is clear that those deans interviewed and surveyed are competent, devoted individuals whose priorities are teaching and learning. It is also clear that an effective dean can increase the effectiveness of both the faculty and the top administration. Based upon this study, the future of the community college is a bright one if the current deans are indicative of what that future is to be.

# APPENDICES

APPENDICES

# Appendix 1

## Questionnaire Used in National Survey of Deans (CLS)

■

DIRECTIONS: In each section, please provide the information or check the spaces as appropriate.

I.  **INSTITUTIONAL INFORMATION:**
    a. State: _____
    b. Number of FTE students—fall 1986 quarter/semester: _____

II. **PERSONAL INFORMATION:**
    a. Number of years in present position: _____
    b. Marital Status:  ( ) Single      ( ) Divorced
                        ( ) Married    ( ) Widowed
                        ( ) Separated
    c. Age: _____ Sex: ( ) Male ( ) Female
       Race: ( ) Black       ( ) Caucasian
             ( ) Hispanic    ( ) Other _____
    d. Do you now live in the state where you finished high school?
       ( ) Yes    ( ) No
    e. Including your current position, how many community college
       deanships have you held? _____

f. Position held *prior* to becoming a community college academic dean:
( ) Division chair       ( ) Dean of Student Services
( ) Faculty member     ( ) Dean of Community Services
( ) Other _____

g. Highest degree held:
( ) Bachelor's    ( ) Ph.D.     ( ) Ed. Specialist
( ) Master's     ( ) Ed.D.     ( ) Other _____

h. Major field of study in your highest degree:
( ) Higher Education    ( ) Other Education _____
( ) Other _____

i. Check the following organizations you belong to:
( ) Kiwanis    ( ) Jaycees    ( ) Masons    ( ) Rotary
( ) Lions     ( ) Ruritan    ( ) Other _____

j. Do you belong to a country club?    ( ) Yes   ( ) No
If 'Yes,' do you use it for professional entertaining?
( ) Yes     ( ) No

k. Time permitting, which of the following sports do you participate in on a regular basis?
( ) Fishing     ( ) Golf      ( ) Hunting    ( ) Jogging
( ) Bowling    ( ) Skiing     ( ) Swimming ( ) Tennis
( ) Other _____
Have you used sports for work-related entertaining in the last 12 months?    ( ) Yes ( ) No

l. Father's most recent full-time occupation: _____

m. Father's highest degree:
( ) None           ( ) Master's
( ) High School     ( ) Doctorate
( ) Associate      ( ) Other _____
( ) Bachelor's

n. Mother's most recent full-time occupation: _____

o. Mother's highest degree:
( ) None           ( ) Master's
( ) High School     ( ) Doctorate
( ) Associate      ( ) Other _____
( ) Bachelor's

p. Check the following organizations you belong to:
( ) AAHE ( ) AERA ( ) NASPA ( ) ASHE ( ) APCA
( ) PDK    ( ) NACUBO    ( ) Other _____

q. State the most recent year you conducted research: _____

r. State the year of your most recent publication: _____
Check the type of publication it was:
( ) book              ( ) book review
( ) article          ( ) book chapter
( ) other _____
If it was in a journal, which one? _____
s. Who is your chief confidant—that is, if you have a major problem on campus to whom do you *first turn?* _____
t. Excluding yourself, whom would you consider the top *two* community college academic deans in your state?

NAME                 COLLEGE

_____

_____

u. Does the chief student services administrator report directly to you? ( ) Yes   ( ) No
v. How likely are you to move to another position within the next five years?
( ) Very likely    ( ) Somewhat likely    ( ) Not likely
w. Is your career goal to be a community college president?
( ) Yes   ( ) No
If "Yes," within how many years do you think you will achieve your goal of becoming a president? _____

## III. SPOUSE: (Skip to Section IV if you are not currently married.)
a. Age _____
b. Highest degree held: ( ) None      ( ) Master's
                    ( ) High School  ( ) Doctorate
                    ( ) Associate    ( ) Other _____
                    ( ) Bachelor's
c. Does your spouse work for pay outside the home? ( ) Yes ( ) No
If your answer is 'Yes,' is the position
_____ full-time    _____ part-time
d. Occupation: _____
e. Has he/she ever obtained a community college degree?
( ) Yes   ( ) No
f. How many years of your married life, while you have been dean, has your spouse worked outside the home? _____

## IV. CHILDREN: (Skip to Section V if you do not have any children.)

a. Number of children under 18 years old: ___ ; 18 and over: ___

b. Of those under 18, how many plan to receive a degree at a
   ____ community college          ____ 4-year public institution
   ____ 4-year private institution    ____ Uncertain

c. Of those 18 and over, how many currently attend or received a degree at a
   ____ community college          ____ 4-year public institution
   ____ 4-year private institution

## V. LIFESTYLE:

We are interested in how many *waking* hours you and your spouse, if married, average in several activities. Because it is difficult to remember exactly how much time was spent in any one activity, ten-hour blocks of time have been listed below. Place one of these estimates in each of the blanks in Questions a and b. For example, if you work 40 hours per week, put "31–40" beside "Work" in Question a.

     0–10    11–20    21–30    31–40    41–50    50+

a. How many hours are spent weekly in the following activities?
   *You*                          *Spouse*
   ____ Work (Include profes-      ____ Work (Include profes-
   sional entertaining)            sional entertaining)
   ____ Family                     ____ Family
   ____ Community Service          ____ Community Service

b. If married, how many hours per week do you and your spouse spend alone together outside of sleeping? _____
   (Skip if unmarried)

c. Check the types of friends you see socially (at least 30 minutes per week) outside of work.
   ( ) childhood friends    ( ) colleagues    ( ) neighbors
   ( ) club associates      ( ) church        ( ) other

d. If married, check the types of friends your spouse sees socially (at least 30 minutes per week) outside of work. (Skip if unmarried)
   ( ) childhood friends    ( ) colleagues    ( ) neighbors
   ( ) club associates      ( ) church        ( ) other

e. How many days of annual leave do you earn each year? \_\_\_\_
f. How many days of annual leave did you take last year? \_\_\_\_
g. Did your family (or you, if unmarried) take a vacation together last year which lasted 4 or more days? ( ) Yes ( ) No
h. If you took a vacation, did you take any work with you?
( ) Yes ( ) No

# Appendix 2

## *Questionnaire Used in Survey of Female, Black, and Hispanic Deans*

■

DIRECTIONS: Please provide the information or check the spaces as appropriate.

1. State: _____
2. Number of FTE students—fall, 1988, quarter/semester: _____
3. Number of years in present position: _____
4. Sex    ( ) Male ( ) Female
5. Marital Status:    ( ) Single        ( ) Divorced
                     ( ) Married       ( ) Widowed
                     ( ) Separated
6. Race: _____
7. Age: _____
8. Do you now live in the state where you finished high school?
   ( ) Yes ( ) No
9. Position held immediately prior to becoming a dean of instruction:
   ( ) Dean or director of community services
   ( ) Dean of administration-finance
   ( ) Dean of student services
   ( ) Division chair
   ( ) Faculty member
   ( ) Other _____

10. Highest degree held:    ( ) Bachelor's                  ( ) Ph.D.
                                 ( ) Master's                  ( ) Ed.D.
                                 ( ) Education Specialist
                                 ( ) Other

11. Major field of study in your highest degree:
    ( ) Higher Education
    ( ) Other Education _____
    ( ) Other (what field) _____

12. Father's most recent full-time occupation: _____

13. Father's highest degree or diploma:
    ( ) None           ( ) Master's
    ( ) High School    ( ) Doctor's
    ( ) Associate      ( ) Other _____
    ( ) Bachelor's

14. Mother's most recent full-time occupation: _____

15. Mother's highest degree:
    ( ) None           ( ) Master's
    ( ) High School    ( ) Doctor's
    ( ) Associate      ( ) Other _____
    ( ) Bachelor's

16. What major obstacles did you encounter on your pathway to the dean of instruction's position that you feel resulted from being a woman (Black, Hispanic)? Please list the obstacles in order of their importance, with the most difficult one first.

17. Did being a woman (Black, Hispanic) help you in obtaining an interview(s) for the deanship? That is, were you included in the pool of applicants because those conducting the search process wanted a woman (Black, Hispanic) applicant? Please explain.

18. Do you feel that affirmative action programs aided you in becoming a dean? _____ yes; _____ no. If yes, please explain.

19. Was the fact that you are a woman (Black, Hispanic) an asset in obtaining your first deanship? _____ yes; _____ no. If yes, please explain.

20. Did you have a mentor who aided you in becoming a dean? If so, was the mentor _____ male; _____ female; _____ Black; _____ Hispanic; _____ white; _____ other?

21. If you had a mentor, what position did he or she hold at the time of the greatest influence over you?

22. Did you have a role model who influenced your career? (Your role model and mentor may have been the same person; however, you may have had a role model who took very little interest in your career yet was someone you looked to as an example.) _____ yes; my mentor; _____ no; _____ yes, someone other than my mentor.

    If you had a role model other than your mentor, was this person _____ female; _____ male; _____ Black; _____ Hispanic; _____ white; _____ other. What position did the role model occupy?

23. Did you have a "negative role model" who built in you a desire to become a dean in order that you could do things differently from how the "negative role model" had done them? _____ yes; _____ no. Was the "negative role model" _____ Black; _____ Hispanic; _____ white? If yes, what position did the person occupy and what were the negative characteristics which caused you to want to be dean in order to correct some of the wrongs this individual may have committed?

24. Were you a member of a peer group (peer network) that aided you in becoming a dean? _____ yes; _____ no.

25. If the answer to No. 24 was yes, was the peer group predominantly
_____ female; _____ male; _____ Black; _____ Hispanic; _____ white;
_____ other.

26. What were your most important non-professional contacts external
to the campus which helped you to become a dean? (E.g., the Chamber of Commerce, etc.) Please list the most important first.

27. What were the most important professional associations and organizations that aided you to become a dean? (E.g., AAUW, AAHE,
AACJC, etc.)

28. Did you participate in a program designed to develop leaders (or at
least enhance leadership skills) prior to becoming a dean? _____ yes;
_____ no. If yes, which of the following did you attend?
_____ ACE Fellows Program
_____ Harvard's IEM;
_____ Bryn Mawr's HERS;
_____ ACE's National Identification Program;
_____ Executive Leadership Institute (League for Innovation and
University of Texas);
_____ Leaders for the 80s;
_____ Other(s); *please list.*

29. During the interview for the dean's position (the one resulting in your
current position) were you asked any questions that were related to
your being a woman (Black, Hispanic)? _____ yes; _____ no. If so, please
give as many examples of the type of questions you were asked that
you can recall. Who asked the questions? (faculty, trustees, etc.)

30. Were you asked any questions related to your being a woman (Black, Hispanic) in any interviews in which you either were not offered the position, or you did not accept the position if offered? _____ yes; _____ no. If so, please give examples of the type of questions you were asked. Who asked the questions? (faculty, trustees, etc.)

31. Prior to becoming a dean, were you ever turned down for a dean's position? _____ yes; _____ no.

32. If yes, did you feel that being a woman (Black, Hispanic) candidate was part of the reason you were turned down? Explain.

33. During the interview process, did you find being a woman (Black, Hispanic) an asset or a liability? _____ yes; _____ no. Please explain either position, or both, if that was the case.

34. Was the role of the spouse of the dean discussed with you during the interview? _____ yes; _____ no. If yes, please describe the discussion.

35. Did you have any particular job assignment that you feel prepared you for the dean's position? _____ yes; _____ no. (Not position, but a specific role; e.g., selling an idea, building a major budget, etc.).

Now that you are dean:
1. Clark Kerr suggests that once a woman becomes a college or university president, she is evaluated on how well she performs and not on the fact that she is a female president. In essence, once someone assumes the presidency, the assessment of performance becomes asexual. Using Kerr's analysis, one might conclude that once someone assumes the presidency, the position is asexual ("aracial"). Do you feel that *once you became a dean*, the position is asexual ("aracial")? _____ yes; _____ no. If no, please explain how the assessment of the position is different for you because you are a woman (Black, Hispanic).

2. In line with the above, are there certain aspects of the dean's position that are *more difficult* because you are a woman (Black, Hispanic)? ____ yes; ____ no. If yes, please explain.

   Are certain aspects of the dean's position *easier* because you are a woman (Black, Hispanic)? ____ yes; ____ no. If yes, please explain.

3. Including your current position, how many deans of instruction's positions have you held? ____.

4. What three most important pieces of advice do you offer to other women (Blacks, Hispanics) who have the dean of instruction's position as a career goal?
   (1)

   (2)

   (3)

5. Is your goal to become a community college president? ____ yes; ____ no. If yes, list the three major obstacles you see facing you *resulting from being a woman* (Black, Hispanic) in moving into a presidency.
   (1)

   (2)

   (3)

OPTIONAL. I will be calling some of the respondents for a *very short* (5–10 minutes) interview. If you would be willing to talk with me for a few minutes, please print your name and telephone number. Thank you.

Name: _____

Day Phone (_____) _____

# Appendix 3

## *Questionnaire Used in Survey of Deans Identified by Their Peers as Outstanding*

■

DIRECTIONS: In sections I and II, please provide the information or check the space as appropriate.

I.  **INSTITUTIONAL INFORMATION**
    a.  State: _____
    b.  Number of FTE students—fall, 1989, quarter/semester: _____

II. **PERSONAL INFORMATION**
    a.  Number of years in present position: _____
    b.  Marital Status:    ( ) Single       ( ) Divorced
                           ( ) Married      ( ) Widowed
                           ( ) Separated
    c.  Age: _____
    d.  Sex: ( ) Female ( ) Male
    e.  Race: ( ) white; ( ) Black; ( ) Hispanic; ( ) other: _____
    f.  Do you now live in the state where you finished high school?
        ( ) Yes ( ) No
    g.  Including your present position, how many community college
        dean of instruction positions have you held? _____

## III. PERSONAL ATTRIBUTES
DIRECTIONS: Please rate responses according to the following scale:

1 = of no importance
2 = of little importance
3 = of considerable importance
4 = of extreme importance
5 = absolutely mandatory

Please rate attributes in terms of their importance to being a successful community college dean of instruction.

____ a. tolerance for ambiguity
____ b. courage to make tough decisions
____ c. physically healthy
____ d. sense of humor
____ e. good judgment
____ f. high intelligence
____ g. loyalty to your college
____ h. concern for others
____ i. flexibility
____ j. charisma
____ k. integrity

____ l. drive or high energy level
____ m. commitment to the community college philosophy
____ n. desire to excel
____ o. curiosity
____ p. optimism
____ q. at ease in different social situations
____ r. willing to take risks
____ s. other, please state:

_____

## IV. SKILLS AND ABILITIES
DIRECTIONS: Please rate responses according to the following scale:

1 = of no importance
2 = of little importance
3 = of considerable importance
4 = of extreme importance
5 = absolutely mandatory

Please rate skills and abilities in terms of their importance to being a successful community college dean of instruction.

____ a. effective communication skills
____ b. delegation of responsibilities
____ c. processing and management of information
____ d. relating well to a broad range of people
____ e. ability to resolve conflicts effectively
____ f. ability to see and take opportunities as they occur
____ g. ability to define problems and offer solutions

___ h. an understanding of the community/region served
___ i. effective articulation of the college's mission and needs
___ j. establishing and maintaining a peer network
___ k. ability to produce scholarly publications
___ l. ability to produce results
___ m. ability to work as a team member
___ n. independence in carrying out programs and duties
___ o. ability to analyze, synthesize, and evaluate
___ p. ability to motivate others
___ q. ability to select capable people
___ r. other, please state: _____

## V. SKILLS AND ABILITIES OF SUBORDINATES

DIRECTIONS: Please rate responses according to the following scale:

1 = of no importance
2 = of little importance
3 = of considerable importance
4 = of extreme importance
5 = absolutely mandatory

Please rate skills and abilities that you generally look for in those who report directly to you.

___ a. effective communication skills
___ b. delegation of responsibilities
___ c. processing and management of information
___ d. relating well to a broad range of people
___ e. ability to resolve conflicts effectively
___ f. ability to see and take opportunities as they occur
___ g. ability to define problems and offer solutions
___ h. an understanding of the community/region served
___ i. effective articulation of the college's mission and needs
___ j. establishing and maintaining a peer network
___ k. ability to produce scholarly publications
___ l. ability to produce results
___ m. ability to work as a team member
___ n. independence in carrying out programs and duties
___ o. ability to analyze, synthesize, and evaluate
___ p. ability to motivate others
___ q. ability to select capable people
___ r. other, please state _____

DIRECTIONS: This next section will attempt to identify the various roles that community college deans of instruction perceive themselves as having. Please check the response that describes the *major* role you play for each question. (*Check one:*)

1. Your principal role with *faculty* is that of:
___ a. colleague
___ b. overall supervisor
___ c. symbol of the college
___ d. articulator and advocate of college's mission and goals
___ e. educational leader
___ f. motivator
___ g. mentor
___ h. role model
___ i. other, please state: _____

2. Your principal role with *those who report directly to you* is that of:
___ a. colleague
___ b. supervisor
___ c. symbol of the college
___ d. articulator and advocate of college's mission and goals
___ e. motivator
___ f. role model
___ g. mentor
___ h. other, please state: _____

3. Your principal role with *students* is that of:
___ a. symbol of authority
___ b. articulator of the college's mission and standards
___ c. role model
___ d. interested, concerned adult
___ e. other, please state: _____

DIRECTIONS: Below are two questions of a general nature. Please check the appropriate response. (*Check one:*)

1. Do you consider the community college dean of instruction position to be a:
___ low-risk position
___ moderate-risk position
___ high-risk position

2. Do you feel that your workload is:
___ heavy ___ average ___ light

DIRECTIONS: Please provide a short written response to the following four questions. Feel free to use another sheet of paper for your answers.

1. Historically, community college professionals (faculty and administrators) have devoted little time to scholarship. If you agree, why do you think this has been true?

2. Based upon my own observations, it seems to me as if there is a new awareness of the role scholarship can and should play in carrying out the community college mission. If you agree with this statement, what is creating this new awareness?

3. If you do not agree with the above statement, why do you think I am wrong?

4. What are you, as your institution's academic leader, doing to promote scholarship on your campus?

Name _____

Address _____

_____

Day Phone (_____) _____

THANK YOU VERY MUCH

# References

■

AACJC Commission on the Future of Community Colleges. *Building Communities: A Vision for a New Century.* Washington, D.C.: American Association of Community and Junior Colleges, 1988.

Anderson, W.H. "Characteristics, Preparation, and Attitudes of Selected Public Junior-Community College Deans of Instruction." Carbondale: Southern Illinois University, 1973. 13 pages. (ED 100 421)

Brown, D.G. (ed.), *Leadership Roles of Chief Academic Officers.* New Directions for Higher Education, no. 47. San Francisco: Jossey-Bass, 1984.

Edgerton, R. "Report From the President." *AAHE Bulletin,* Vol. 41, No. 10. American Association for Higher Education, June, 1989.

Green, M.F. *The American College President: A Contemporary Profile.* Center for Leadership Development. Washington, D.C.: American Council on Education, 1988.

Kerr, C. and Gade, M. *The Many Lives of Academic Presidents.* Washington, D. C.: Association of Governing Boards of Universities and Colleges, 1986.

Marchese, T. "The Chief Academic Officer: An Interview with Richard I. Miller." *AAHE Bulletin,* Vol. 41, No. 6, American Association for Higher Education, February, 1989.

Orfield, Gary. "Hispanics." In Arthur Levine (ed.), *Shaping Higher Education's Future: Demographic Realities and Opportunities, 1990–2000.* San Francisco: Jossey-Bass, 1989.

Parker, P. and Parker, P.W. "Instructional Leadership: A Profile of Chief Academic Officers in Kansas Community Colleges." Pittsburg State University, KS, 1985. 18 pages. (ED 254 271)

Puyear, D., Perkins, J. and Vaughan, G.B. "The Community College Dean of Instruction." *Community, Technical, and Junior College Journal,* April–May, 1990.

Reinhard, B. "AACJC Emphasizing Minority Education in its 1990 Public Policy Agenda Plans." *The Community, Technical, and Junior College Times,* August 29, 1989, p. 4.

Roueche, J., Baker, G., and Rose, R. *Shared Vision: Transformational Leadership in American Community Colleges.* Washington, D.C.: The Community College Press, 1989.

Shawl, W.F. *The Role of the Academic Dean.* Topical Paper No. 42. Los Angeles: ERIC Clearinghouse for Junior Colleges, 1974.

Thomas, G.E. and Hirsch, D.J. "Blacks." In Arthur Levine (ed.), *Shaping Higher Education's Future: Demographic Realities and Opportunities, 1990–2000.* San Francisco: Jossey-Bass, 1989.

Vaughan, G.B. "Community Services: Pathway to the Presidency?" *The Community Services Catalyst,* Spring, 1987.

Vaughan, G.B. "Female Community College Presidents." *Community College Review,* Fall, 1989a.

Vaughan, G.B. *Leadership in Transition: The Community College Presidency.* New York: ACE/Macmillan, 1989b.

Vaughan, G.B. *The Community College Presidency.* New York: ACE/Macmillan, 1986.

Vaughan, G.B. "Scholarship in Community Colleges: The Path to Respect." *Educational Record,* Spring, 1988.

Weintraub, R.G. "Ten Caveats for Presidential Candidates." *Academic News,* May, 1987.

Wheelan, B. "Who Am I?" in *Jump at the Sun: Perspectives of Black Women Administrators.* Annandale, VA: Northern Virginia Community College, n/d.

Wolverton, R.E. "The Chief Academic Officer: Argus on the Campus." In David G. Brown (ed.), *Leadership Roles of Chief Academic Officers.* New Directions for Higher Education, no. 47. San Francisco, Jossey-Bass, 1984.

# Index

■